SKILLS AND VALUES: CONSTITUTIONAL LAW

SKILLS AND VALUES: CONSTITUTIONAL LAW

William D. Araiza
Professor of Law
Brooklyn Law School

Thomas E. Baker
Professor of Law
Florida International University College of Law

Olympia Duhart
Professor of Law and Director of Lawyering Skills & Values Program
Nova Southeastern University, Shepard Broad Law School

Steven I. Friedland
Professor of Law and Senior Scholar
Elon University School of Law

ISBN: 978-1-4224-7451-8 (print)
ISBN: 978-0-3271-7963-4 (eBook)

Library of Congress Cataloging-in-Publication Data

Araiza, William D.
  Skills and values. Constitutional law / William D. Araiza, Professor of Law, Brooklyn Law School [and three others].
    pages cm.
    Includes index.
    ISBN 978-1-4224-7451-8
  1. Constitutional law—United States—Problems, exercises, etc. I. Title. II. Title: Constitutional law.
  KF4550.Z9A47 2013
  342.73—dc23

                                                                                    2013007551

This publication is designed to provide authoritative information in regard to the subject matter covered. It is sold with the understanding that the publisher is not engaged in rendering legal, accounting, or other professional services. If legal advice or other expert assistance is required, the services of a competent professional should be sought.

NOTE TO USERS
To ensure that you are using the latest materials available in this area, please be sure to periodically check the LexisNexis Law School web site for downloadable updates and supplements at www.lexisnexis.com/lawschool.

Editorial Offices
121 Chanlon Rd., New Providence, NJ 07974 (908) 464-6800
201 Mission St., San Francisco, CA 94105-1831 (415) 908-3200
www.lexisnexis.com

MATTHEW◆BENDER

ACKNOWLEDGEMENTS

Professor Araiza would like to thank his research assistants: Jing Jin, Kristie LaSalle, Meir Lax, and Michael Teitel. He also thanks Gloria Kern for her general assistance, and acknowledges the support of Dean Nicholas Allard.

Professor Baker is especially grateful for the helpful efforts of his research assistants: Keoki Baron, Andrea M. Canona, Alexander Martini, and Dick M. Ortega. He also thanks Veronica Torres for her general assistance. Finally, he appreciates the support of Dean R. Alex Acosta and the FIU College of Law.

Professor Duhart would like to thank her research assistant Lydia Harley for her thoughtful edits and assistance on this project. She is also very grateful to her faculty assistant Joseph H. Baldelomar for his dedication and support.

Professor Friedland would like to thank my research assistant, Susanna Guffy and library liaison, Lisa Watson, for their dedicated and unwavering efforts to improve my work product, and faculty assistant Kristin Walker for her work and ability to keep smiling during the most wretched computer snafus. All errors, ambiguities and inconsistencies in my work are definitely my responsibility.

INTRODUCTION

These materials are intended to provide an opportunity to use various lawyering skills within the context of a Constitutional Law course. We have designed the problems around active learning — it will be up to you to solve the analytical issues while using specific skills. A concurrent goal with the deployment of skills is that by working through the exercises, you should be able to supplement and enhance your understanding of the substantive Constitutional Law material as well.

Each chapter is cabined by a substantive law area. Within these areas you will find exercises by which you will be able to apply your knowledge of the constitutional law rules using a variety of skills. Each exercise focuses on a particular doctrinal rule or rules. You must transfer your knowledge of the subject to a particular fact setting — but generally not by merely answering a legal question directly. Instead, you might be asked to draft a statute, write a complaint, compose a motion to dismiss, take a deposition or do other lawyer-specific tasks. You also will be asked to represent particular clients — take sides — as well as serve as a judge.

Each exercise offers an opportunity to track your performance and obtain ready and particularized feedback. Feedback is very helpful in determining whether you are progressing in your level of knowledge and your and skills. The student notes offer the authors' ideas about the issues, but it is important to emphasize that these are not the only way to respond to the questions. Instead, the notes offer at least one way to analyze the questions presented.

Since Constitutional Law is a second semester course in your first year of law school or offered in the second year, you likely already know that how your professor approaches the substantive issues is controlling — not our approach. One additional matter — the self-assessments, found on the LexisNexis Web Course, are designed to help you after you have worked through the problems and are not there to provide some assistance in advance. It will defeat the purpose if you decide to run through the exercises backwards, looking at the self-assessments before attempting your own analysis. Besides, some people need to muck about with issues for a while before the light bulb goes off and their learning reaches a new threshold. That could be you.

The LexisNexis Web Course also has additional material and information. Our goal with this book was to provide tools to assist you throughout the learning process, and some of these tools were best deployed on the LexisNexis Web Course.

Each chapter includes the following components:

- *Introduction to the substantive law.* These introductions provide an overview and review of the doctrinal areas covered by the exercises. We have thrown in some commentary as well, trying to dig beneath the surface of the rules.
- *Your Role in the Exercise.* You could be any one of a number of individuals involved in a problem, from a private lawyer, to a government lawyer, to offering advice to a group to serving as a judge or expert.
- *Required Tasks.* This component describes what it is you will be asked to do, from

writing a memorandum, to taking a deposition, writing a motion or providing advice.

- *Practice Skills Utilized.* The particular skills needed to respond to the question will be listed in the problem so you can have an idea in advance of what tools will be needed to solve the problem.

- *Time for Completion and Level of Difficulty.* Each exercise has its own time-table and rating for a level of difficulty. While these are subjective, it is in keeping with the theme of this book, and that is to provide as much express guidance as possible.

We hope you find this supplement useful and worthwhile. Given the push toward integrating skills in traditional substantive courses, we eagerly wanted to provide at least a small opportunity to students to experience lawyering skills at an early stage of law school.

William D. Araiza
Thomas E. Baker
Olympia Duhart
Steven I. Friedland

TABLE OF CONTENTS

TABLE OF CONTENTS

Chapter 1

A PREREQUISITE TO CONSTITUTIONAL ISSUES: STATE ACTION

INTRODUCTION

This chapter addresses the critical requirement for "state action" that must be present to support any and every constitutional claim. The Constitution's guarantees for due process and equal protection and all its protection of individual liberties are a central component in any Constitutional Law course, and more importantly, in the protection of individual liberty in the real world. However, these important Constitutional guarantees only apply to the government. Therefore, only the "state" is bound by the Constitution. Generally, the Constitution does not apply to private actors.

Furthermore, the term "state" should be viewed expansively. It is not merely limited to a state government or government officer. Instead, it applies to any local, state, or federal government actor. For example, a police officer, a city commissioner, a county manager, a local school board, a public school teacher, a state governor, a federal agency or Congress would all qualify as "state" actors when they are performing their official duties, i.e., acting "under color of law." Challenged action that is advanced by statute, ordinance or any other type of legislative act obviously involves the "state." Furthermore, rulings from administrative and regulatory agencies, as well as judicial action by courts, qualify as state action. The requirement that the Constitution's protections of individual liberties be limited to conduct asserted by a government officer is known as the "state action doctrine."

Is the requirement for state action sound interpretation of the Fourteenth Amendment? This question has challenged the Court for more than a hundred years as it has wrestled with the important competing interests of individual autonomy and the protection of basic rights. As you work through the material on the state action requirement, keep this tension in mind.

There are, of course, some notable exceptions to this requirement. First, the 13th Amendment to the Constitution is unique in its direct application to private conduct. On its face, Section 1 of the 13th Amendment forbids people from being or owning slaves: "Neither slavery, nor involuntary servitude, except as a punishment for crime whereof the party shall have been duly convicted, shall exist within the United States, or any place subject to their jurisdiction."

While not technically an exception to the state action doctrine, Constitutional norms also can reach private conduct through the application of federal or state law. That is, private actors that would generally be beyond the reach of the Constitution can be held to equal protection guarantees, and others, because of a federal or state statute that governs private conduct. For instance, the Civil Rights Act of 1964 outlaws discrimination on the basis of race, color, religion or national origin in public accommodations such as hotels, motels, restaurants and theaters.

Finally, a few state action doctrines arise under very specific circumstances. Because the circumstances would extend the protection of the Constitution to private individuals — and beyond the government — these doctrines have generally been narrowly defined. These doctrines describe situations when the linkage between the private actors and the state is close enough to fairly and constitutionally attribute otherwise private conduct to the state itself and trigger the application of the Constitution. The two primary examples that have gained recognition are the public function exception and the entanglement exception. Both exceptions seem to support the constitutional policy concerns for restricting private actors from violating basic rights when actors assume the role of a government actor or become virtually indistinguishable from a government actor.

Under the public function exception, a private actor that exercises a power traditionally exclusively reserved for the state has satisfied the public function exception. The Supreme Court has held that private individuals or groups who are "endowed by the State with powers or functions governmental in nature" effectively serve as "instrumentalities of the State" and are therefore "subject to its constitutional limitations." *Evans v. Newton*, 382 U.S. 296, 299 (1966). Examples of this exception include private companies running prisons or private civic organizations staging an election.

The second exception to the state action requirement is the entanglement exception. The entanglement exception transforms private conduct into state action (and triggers Fourteenth Amendment scrutiny) when the government's involvement facilitates the challenged conduct. Minimum government involvement with the private actor is not enough; rather, the government must authorize or encourage the unconstitutional conduct. The big question here, then, is how much involvement is enough to trigger the state action doctrine?

When a plaintiff asserts a violation of an individual liberty, then, the first inquiry should be whether a "state actor" is involved. Absent the application of state or federal law, or an exception to the "state action doctrine," private actors are typically not bound by the Constitution. For example, a private club does not violate the First Amendment by restricting speech.

Once the private actor has been qualified as a "state actor" under one of the exceptions, the attorney can move on to analyzing the underlying constitutional claim. Remember, resolution of the state action doctrine is only step one of the problem for a practicing attorney.

EXERCISE 1.1: THE COMPANY TOWN AND THE CARE FACILITY

SUBSTANTIVE CONTENT:

- Introduction to state action doctrine
- Public function exception
- Entanglement exception

SKILLS AND VALUES UTILIZED:

- Fact analysis and development
- Creative problem solving
- Collaborative problem solving
- Drafting a portion of an interoffice memorandum

GENERAL DESCRIPTION OF EXERCISE:

Task 1: "Outlining the Issues" — You are tasked here with developing a strategy that will advance a claim for plaintiff challenging possible private conduct for violating equal protection.

Task 2: "Drafting a Memo" — Your team is charged with researching, drafting and delivering the Discussion section of an interoffice memorandum.

PARTICIPANTS NEEDED:

Task 1 is an individual project

Task 2 is a collaborative project, involving teams of 2 to 5 students

ESTIMATED TIME FOR COMPLETION:

Task 1: 1 hour

Task 2: One-half hour to prepare and one to two hours for your group to meet and discuss, draft and then summarize the discussion for the entire class, if required by professor.

LEVEL OF DIFFICULTY (1 to 5):

ROLE IN EXERCISE: You are acting as a lawyer for a pro bono client, Lucy Newton, who wants to bring a lawsuit against a private company that owns and manages a company town. She is also considering a possible suit against the owner of a local urgent care facility.

TASK 1: Outlining a Complaint.

You have just started your first position as an attorney in the downtown Miami office of Legal Aid. Your first pro bono client is a woman named Lucy Newton, an advocate for local homeless shelters and a volunteer in the nonprofit organization Helping Hands. A client interview with Ms. Newton has revealed the following information:

Helping Hands has recently launched a three-month drive to raise awareness about the burden of homelessness that is plaguing new Haitian immigrants. Ms. Newton is one of several volunteers dispatched to communities throughout South Florida to distribute flyers about homeless immigrants and collect donations to fund Creole-language initiatives providing resources that are available for homeless people. The Helping Hands organization is organized and supported by a local Catholic parish that Ms. Newton attends.

As part of the assigned neighborhood trek, she recently visited Millennial Village, a community on Biscayne Bay. Millennial Village is owned by the Bayview Sailing Corporation, and is primarily home to employees of the luxury sailboat manufacturer. The company owns the village and runs all aspects of the village. The community consists of a strip mall, on which business places are situated, paved streets, a system of sewers, a sewage disposal plant, more than two dozen residential buildings and sidewalks located along the street. One small building is used by the United States as a post-office. There is also a deputy of Dade County Police stationed in the town, though her salary is paid by the Bayview Sailing Corporation. The village is accessible to both highway traffic and pedestrians, since there is no gate separating the community from the surrounding neighborhood. There are, however, several signs posted throughout the village.

Each sign reads:

> **This is Private**
> **Property.**
> **No solicitation of**
> **any kind will be**
> **permitted.**

Ms. Newton admitted that she saw the one of these signs as she walked along a sidewalk near the post-office in Millennial Village. Nevertheless, she proceeded to distribute flyers about the Helping Hands initiative and her parish church. Within an hour, she was warned that she could not distribute any flyers in Millennial Village. She said she told the sheriff that she was within her rights to distribute religious writings and that she refused to leave. When she was warned a second time and refused, she was arrested. Ms. Newton, who has since been released, wants to bring a lawsuit against Millennial Village asserting a violation of her First Amendment rights.

Before you proceed, you need to first resolve the issue of whether this conduct qualifies as state action. Can Millennial Village be sued for a Constitutional violation? In drafting the complaint, which facts will you emphasize and why? First, write a list of the key facts from the interview that you will rely on in the complaint. Do you think this conduct by Millennial Village violates the Constitution? Is it government conduct or "state action"? If so, which exception to the state action doctrine will you assert? Can you identify any United States Supreme Court cases that will support your assertion that the conduct of Millennial Village qualifies as one of the exceptions to the state action doctrine? Write one paragraph outlining your approach for the complaint.

TASK 2: Drafting an Interoffice Memorandum.

Before you joined Legal Aid, Ms. Newton was working with another attorney on a separate issue. She was interested in bringing a lawsuit against FastFix, a privately-owned urgent care facility in her community. The previous attorney had already started drafting an interoffice memorandum on the FastFix issue, but took a leave before he could finish the memo when he and his wife adopted a young child.

You have been asked to complete the predictive memorandum on the possible complaint against FastFix. (A copy of the incomplete memo is attached below.) As you will see from the working draft of the memorandum, the primary issue is whether FastFix's discriminatory business practices qualify as state action under one of the exceptions to the state action doctrine.

Your task is to draft the Brief Answer and Discussion sections of the memo. Write out logical responses to this preliminary issue; support with relevant case law. Limit your response to five sentences.

In crafting the Brief Answer, follow the suggested format: 1) A brief answer on the question presented; 2) a summary of the law in the jurisdiction (include any relevant limits or exceptions); 3) a concise application of law to facts. Generally, no cites are needed in the Brief Answer. The function of the Brief Answer is to give the busy attorney a quick snapshot of the prediction generated by the interoffice memorandum.[1]

The Discussion section of the memorandum can take many formats. Speak with your team members and adapt the organizational format you are most comfortable using.

INTEROFFICE MEMORANDUM

To: Sabrina Chen, Director, Legal Aid of Miami

From: New Attorney

Re: Client Lucy Newton, Possible Claim against FastFix, Client File #529

Date: Jan. 6, 2012

QUESTION PRESENTED

Under federal law, does a private business constitute a "state actor" when the city in which it is located provides grants to the business, approves of its business plan and actively promotes its policy that restricts delivery of urgent care health care services to American citizens?

BRIEF ANSWER

In this section of the memo, your team must draft a BRIEF ANSWER that responds to the QUESTION PRESENTED. Follow the suggested format for the response. No citations are needed in your response.

FACTS

In October 2011, the City of Miami approved a business permit request for FastFix, an urgent care facility that offered limited general practice medical care for patients. As part of its efforts to lure businesses into a struggling strip mall, the City also offered $10,000 in grants to the privately owned business. The grants were intended to help develop the exterior, signage, and landscaping near the business. Before granting the business permit and cash incentives, the City Commission requested a copy of the company's business plan for review and approval. FastFix, Inc. complied and delivered its complete business plan to both the City Commission and City Manager 20 days before the scheduled vote on the permit.

---

[1] *See* LINDA EDWARDS, LEGAL WRITING: PROCESS, ANALYSIS AND ORGANIZATION (2006).

According to the business plan submitted to the city and approved in its entirety, FastFix limits its care to American citizens. The relevant portions of its business plan reads:

> The owners of FastFix are committed to providing quality, affordable medical care to United States citizens. We "take care of our own" and that begins with ensuring access to urgent health care to those who are able to produce documentation of American citizenship. Health care is not a right, but a privilege. Accordingly, FastFix will only serve patients who are American citizens. Acceptable proof of citizenship will include birth certificates, United States passports, and newly documented driver's licenses that feature the proof of US citizenship seal. Patients without proper proof of citizenship will not be treated by FastFix, Inc.

When questioned by a City Commissioner David Wolde at the October 2011 meeting, FastFix owner Rodney Gills defended the company policy of restricting health care services to United States citizens by citing to the "recent rash of prescription drug abuse" by members of the community. Commissioner Wolde responded that he thought the limitation was "an excellent initiative to curb the abuse of prescription drug mills in the city limits." The City Commission then approved the business plan; the vote was unanimous. In a subsequent meeting, the city awarded FastFix a one-time $10,000 small business grant. From January to March 2012, the city advertised the "We Take Care of Our Own" motto on its cable access channel, and encouraged city residents with proof of US Citizenship to patronize FastFix and other small businesses along the struggling business corridor.

On February 18, 2012, Ms. Lucy Newton visited FastFix with complaints of an ear ache and a low-grade fever. She was immediately asked to produce proof of United States citizenship. Ms. Newton, who is an undocumented immigrant from Haiti, did not have the required paperwork. She was therefore turned away by a desk clerk and refused treatment. (Ms. Newton had to drive 15 miles to another urgent care facility, where she was treated for an ear infection and prescribed antibiotics.) She has asked Legal Aid to determine whether she can bring a claim against FastFix for violating her 14th Amendment rights under the Equal Protection Clause. The threshold issue is whether FastFix, a privately owned business, qualifies as a state actor under one of the established exceptions.

DISCUSSION

In this section of the memo, your team must draft a logical, well-organized discussion that responds in-depth to the Question Presented. Use relevant case law to support your response.

Chapter 2

STANDING AND THE SPENDING POWER

INTRODUCTION

The problem in this chapter concerns both standing and the federal spending power.

Standing:

Standing doctrine asks whether the plaintiff is a proper person to bring the lawsuit. Standing is largely, though not completely, based on Article III's provision that the federal judicial power extends to "cases and controversies": the thought is that there is no proper "case or controversy" if the plaintiff is not the proper person to bring the lawsuit. *See, e.g., Muskrat v. United States*, 219 U.S. 346 (1911).

In its Article III dimension, standing requires that the plaintiff have been injured (or that his injury is imminent), that the injury be caused by the defendant, and that the injury be redressable by a court. Each of these concepts appears straightforward, but carries with it its own ambiguities.

Injury. You might think it's clear what "injury" is, from a legal standpoint: deprivations of common-law protected interests such as bodily integrity (literally, injury!) or property interests. But injury extends beyond that. Aesthetic injury (the loss of a view), the loss of opportunities (e.g., to hike in a pristine wilderness that is being bulldozed), and even the loss of the business and social opportunities provided by living in an integrated environment have all been considered "injury" for Article III purposes. Moreover, Congress can, by statute, create rights, the deprivation of which creates injury for Article III purposes. *See, e.g., Havens Realty Corp. v. Coleman* 455 U.S. 363 (1982) (concluding that in the federal fair housing statute Congress gave every American a right not to be lied to about the availability of housing because of the would-be resident's race).

Given the breadth of this conception of injury, you would think almost anything would constitute injury. Not quite. Simply having a professional interest in a subject is not enough. For example, a specialist in a particular animal species is not injured when that species is threatened by a defendant's conduct. *See Lujan v. Defenders of Wildlife*, 504 U.S. 555 (1992). Moreover, the requirement that the injury be "actual" or "imminent" means that some speculative harms will not count, if they are simply not imminent enough.

Moreover, at times the Court has stated that Article III injury must be personal — that is, a "generalized grievance" does not suffice. For example, in *Defenders of Wildlife* the Court held that plaintiffs were not "injured" in the Article III sense simply because the government failed to comply with the law. For the Court, that type of harm was one shared in equal measure by all Americans; hence it was "generalized." At other times the Court has suggested that some injuries that might be considered as generalized might still be cognizable for standing purposes. *See Federal Election Comm'n v. Akins*, 524 U.S. 11 (1998).

Causation. Causation also appears straightforward. But if you've had Torts you know that it doesn't take much to spin a story out in which causation becomes quite broad. The Court generally insists on a fairly tight causation chain. For example, in *Warth v. Seldin*, 422 U.S. 490 (1975), the Court considered a claim that a town's zoning rules caused low-income persons to be excluded from the chance to live in the town. The Court rejected the plaintiffs' standing argument, concluding that it might have been the economics of the housing market in the town, rather than the zoning ordinance, that kept builders from building low-income housing in the town. As you may recall from Torts, causation is less a science than an art — there is a lot of policy involved in a determination that factor A "caused" effect X.

Redressability. Redressability requires that courts be confident that a ruling in the plaintiff's favor would make the plaintiff whole. This requirement is fundamental to the role of federal courts in our system: they exist to give relief to injured parties, not simply to pass on abstract legal questions. Thus, if a court is unsure whether it can in fact give relief to a plaintiff, it will likely conclude that the injury is not redressable.

Causation and redressability do not have to be proven 100% before a plaintiff has standing. But a court does have to be satisfied that it is likely that the defendant caused the injury, and that the injury would be redressable.

The complexity lurking in these seemingly simple rules was illustrated in *Simon v. E. Kentucky Welfare Rights Org.*, 426 U.S. 26 (1976). In *E. Kentucky* a welfare rights organization sued the IRS, alleging that its rules made it too easy for hospitals to claim charity status while denying free or low-cost health care to poor people. (Charity status is desirable because it allows contributions to the hospital to be tax-deductible.) The Court held the organization had no standing to sue on behalf of indigent would-be patients. It concluded that it wasn't clear whether the IRS's actions had actually caused the denial of care, reasoning that if hospitals were forced to provide more free care in order to preserve their charity status, they might forego that status and deny the care anyway. For this same reason, the Court concluded that an order requiring the IRS to tighten up its charity standards would not likely redress the plaintiff's injury.

Prudential Standing Limits. In addition to Article III standing requirements, the Court has enunciated several "prudential," or policy-based, standing limits. These limits are not based in Article III *per se*, but rather in the courts' view that it makes sense to not allow certain types of plaintiffs to sue. Probably the most important prudential standing limit prevents plaintiffs from suing to assert the legal rights of a third party. For example, in *Warth*, one of the plaintiffs was an association of taxpayers from a neighboring town, whose standing claim was that the defendant-town's zoning ordinance kept poor people out, thus increasing the tax burden on the taxpayers' own town (and thus the taxpayers' tax liability). The Court assumed, for purposes of argument, that the taxpayers had Article III standing, but it concluded that they were asserting the would-be residents' legal right to non-discrimination, in violation of the ban on asserting third-party rights.

Because this ban is prudential — that is, based on policy — both courts and Congress can make exceptions to it if it makes good sense to. For example, the Court has allowed abortion doctors to assert the abortion rights of pregnant women, on the theory that the doctors have a close professional relationship with the women, and that the women can only vindicate their abortion rights by acting through the doctors. *Singleton v. Wulff*, 428 U.S. 106 (1976). Similarly, Congress can make exceptions to this standing limitation, by enacting a statute that gives any citizen a right to sue to enforce that law. Again, these exceptions do not excuse the plaintiffs from having to demonstrate Article III standing. But if they satisfy Article III's requirements, then Congress or the courts may be willing to excuse failure to comply with prudential requirements.

The Spending Power:

Article I gives Congress the power "to pay the Debts and provide for the common Defence and general Welfare of the United States." Art. I § 8, cl. 1. The "spending power" has historically been construed broadly. In *United States v. Butler*, 297 U.S. 1 (1936), the Court held that that power was not limited to spending in pursuance of regulating one of the subject-matter areas that the rest of Article I gives to Congress (e.g., the power to regulate interstate commerce). Instead, the spending power allows Congress to spend even on subjects that it is not authorized to regulate directly. The general breadth of the spending power has not come under question in recent years, even as the Supreme Court has cut back on some of Congress's most important regulatory powers, most notably the power to regulate interstate commerce and to enforce the Fourteenth Amendment. *See, e.g.*, *United States v. Lopez*, 514 U.S. 549 (1995) (commerce power); *City of Boerne v. Flores*, 521 U.S. 507 (1997) (enforcement power).

A particular facet of the spending power that has drawn attention in recent decades is Congress's power to provide money to states, where the grant is conditioned on the state taking certain actions that Congress cannot mandate directly. In *South Dakota v. Dole*, 483 U.S. 203 (1987), the Court considered a challenge to a federal highway statute that granted highway construction money to states, but withheld a small percentage of the funds if the state failed to raise its drinking age to 21. By a 7-2 majority it upheld the law.

The *Dole* Court enunciated a four-factor test for evaluating the constitutionality of such conditional spending grants. First, the spending program must be in pursuit of the general welfare. The Court observed that this requirement was so general that it was doubtful whether courts were capable of policing it. *See Dole*, 483 U.S. at 207 n. 2. Second, the condition must be unambiguously stated in the statute. The point of this requirement was to ensure that the state be on notice that accepting the money obligated it to comply with the condition. *See Dole*, 483 U.S. at 207. Third, the condition had to be related to the federal interest in the spending program. *See id.* The majority noted that South Dakota, the plaintiff in the case, had not alleged that any of these three elements was violated and in particular had not suggested a tighter relatedness requirement. However, in a footnote it left open the door for a tighter relatedness requirement in the future, in which the condition would have to be related to the actual use to which the money was to be put. *See Dole*, 483 U.S. at 208 n. 3. This point is discussed further below, in the context of the 2012 case upholding the federal healthcare law, *National Federation of Independent Business v. Sebelius*, 183 L. Ed. 2d 450 (2012).

Fourth, the condition could not induce the state to violate the Constitution. *See Dole*, 483 U.S. at 208. South Dakota had argued that the highway program failed this requirement, as it allegedly violated the Twenty-First Amendment by imposing federal regulation over alcohol consumption. However, the Court explained that this element referred to inducements to the violation of individual rights, rather than structural provisions, such as which level of government enjoys which regulatory powers. *See Dole*, 483 U.S. at 210-211.

Finally, the *Dole* Court noted the possibility that federal grant programs could be so important to states that attaching conditions on those grants might effectively coerce states to regulate in ways they would not otherwise prefer. However, the Court concluded that the threatened funding cut was such a small part of the overall highway funds grant that it could not be considered coercive. *See Dole*, 483 U.S. at 211.

The Court reached a different result on the coercion issue in *National Federation of Independent Business v. Sebelius*, 183 L. Ed. 2d 450 (2012), the case considering the constitutionality of the comprehensive federal health care law sometimes called the "Affordable Care Act" or "ACA." One part of the ACA provided for a significant expansion of the federal Medicaid program, a federal program that is jointly administered and financed by the federal governments and states that choose to participate. The ACA significantly expanded the availability of Medicaid by making many more categories of persons eligible for Medicaid insurance. As part of that expansion, the ACA committed the federal government to pay 100% of the additional costs the expansion would impose on the states, declining to 90% after 2016. The ACA also provided that states declining to participate in this expansion would lose federal funding for all of their Medicaid expenses.

In *National Federation* seven justices concluded that the threat of a state losing all of its Medicaid funding was sufficiently coercive as to violate the *South Dakota* rule. In two separate opinions, the majority noted the size of the Medicaid program in concluding that states had no realistic option to decline to participate in the ACA's Medicaid expansion. The justices noted that the average states spends at least 20% of its total expenditures on Medicaid, of which the federal government pays at least 50%; thus, the loss of federal Medicaid funds threatened by non-participation in the ACA's Medicaid expansion could deny an average state an amount equal to at least 10% of total annual expenditures. By contrast, in *Dole* the plaintiff state stood to lose less than one half of one percent of its annual expenditures. The Court also rejected the argument that the federal government was merely threatening states with losing money for a program when they failed to comply with federal conditions related to that same program. The Court concluded instead that the ACA's expansion of Medicaid eligibility to entirely new classes of persons effectively rendered that expansion a separate program. Under this reasoning, Congress was coercing states to participate in a "new" program (the Medicaid expansion) by threatening them with the loss of funds for a separate program (the pre-existing Medicaid program).

The line drawn by *National Federation* is, of course, vague. Depending on where to draw it, in terms of the size of the threatened funding withdrawal, will be difficult. Indeed, Medicaid may be unique, given the size of the program. Still, the Court's analysis means that in the future lawyers evaluating the constitutionality of conditional federal grants to the states must consider both the size of any threatened funding cut-off and the relationship of the program whose funding is threatened to the program in which participation is conditionally offered.

EXERCISE 2.1: FEDERAL DOLLARS/FEDERAL LITIGATION

SKILLS AND VALUES UTILIZED:

- Deposition Preparation
- Legal Analysis and Memo Drafting
- Statutory Drafting

GENERAL DESCRIPTION OF EXERCISE:

Task 1: As lawyer for the plaintiff, you will prepare your client for deposition questions you expect the other side to ask him, and that you will want to ask him.

Task 2: You will be asked to write a memo analyzing the likelihood that a court would strike the statute down, and to redraft the statute to minimize that risk.

PARTICIPANTS NEEDED: Both tasks can be accomplished by students working individually. However, it is preferred that students work in groups of 2 or 3.

ESTIMATED TIME FOR COMPLETION: Approximately 1.5 hours

LEVEL OF DIFFICULTY (1 to 5):

ROLE IN EXERCISE: In task 1 you are the attorney for one of the plaintiffs described in the exercise. In task 2 you are a lawyer for the federal government litigating the case against the other plaintiff described in the exercise, and also involved in policy work on this issue.

TASKS: Task 1 requires you to prepare your client for a deposition. Task 2 requires you to analyze the constitutionality of a statute, and to redraft it to minimize the likelihood that it will be struck down.

During a severe economic downturn Congress enacts the "Help America's States Work Act" (HASWA, or Act). The Act reads as follows:

Section 1: Findings

The Congress hereby finds the following:

1. The economic downturn has made it difficult for many state governments to provide the services they normally provide, services that are crucial to the well-being of the American people.

2. Federal money should not be spent to support discriminatory hiring practices that run counter to the fundamental values of the American people.

Section 2: Funds for State Government Employment

There is hereby appropriated $500 million for distribution to the states, on a per capita population basis, for the purpose of subsidizing the hiring of state employees to deliver important state services. In order to qualify for these funds a state shall specify the program(s) for which these funds will be used. The State shall also affirm that it does not engage in invidious employment discrimination of any type and in any program before any such funds will be released.

If any state declines or is deemed ineligible for the funds allocated to it, those funds shall be re-allocated to the accepting and eligible states, on a per capita population basis.

Section 3: Limitations on the Use of Funds

The Department of Labor (DOL, or Department) shall oversee the distribution of HASWA funds in a way that respects state government autonomy. Before releasing funds to a state, the Department shall ensure that a state does not engage in invidious employment discrimination.

Six months after enactment of the statute the DOL issues the following regulation regarding HASWA funds.

Reg 2011-861: States accepting HASWA funds may not engage in any type of discrimination based on race or sex.

These developments cause two parties to want to sue, but for very different reasons.

Plaintiff 1: Joey Johnson: Johnson is a graduate student in the middle of his PhD program in micro-biology at Emory University in Atlanta. His dream job is to work at the Georgia Department of Agriculture, where he has already interned, and where he has a number of contacts. He got excellent reviews during his internship, and, at the farewell lunch for Johnson his supervisor told him that he "should definitely apply for a permanent position when you [Johnson] are ready." Johnson is also a paraplegic, having lost the use of his legs in an accident ten years ago. He uses a wheelchair for mobility.

Johnson is concerned about the federal statute, which he believes implicitly authorizes the State Agriculture Department to maintain its policy of not hiring wheelchair users for "permanent positions that require significant movement as part of normal working activities." *Georgia Dept of Agriculture Personnel Regulation 18-101.* The position Johnson would like to have requires taking soil samples from farm sites, and thus requires travel to the sites and movement around the farms. He also wonders if the possible unavailability of a job with the State of Georgia should cause him to shift his course work and dissertation toward subjects that would be of more use in seeking a job in private industry.

Rather than sue the state, Johnson instead sues the federal government, alleging that the Department of Labor's interpretation of the statute is erroneous. He alleges that Congress intended to ban the distribution of federal funds to states that engage in a variety of discrimination, including discrimination based on disability.

TASK 1: Deposition Preparation.

You are Johnson's lawyer. The court has decided that the two sides may now start deposing witnesses on the question whether Johnson has standing. You now face two sets of questions and two tasks.

a. Who would you like to depose? What information would you hope to elicit from them? Draft a set of questions that would elicit that information.

b. Assuming that the federal government will seek to depose your client, what questions should you advise your client to be ready for? Draft a set of likely questions to give to your client, and explain why it's likely the government lawyers will ask those questions. Consider how you will present these questions to Johnson, keeping in mind a lawyer's ethical obligations regarding "coaching" clients — i.e., prompting or urging them to give particular answers.

Plaintiff 2: The State of Kansas: The State of Kansas has requested HASWA funds for a wide variety of programs including education, environmental protection and emergency preparedness. However, the State has not requested HASWA funds for running its prison system.

The State has a policy of hiring only women for prison guard positions at its State Correctional Facility for Women. It believes that DOL's regulation will prevent it from maintaining this policy, even if it does not use HASWA money to hire prison guards. The State sues the federal government, alleging that it would violate the Constitution for the statute to authorize the federal government to withhold money destined for state programs other than prisons because of the state prison's hiring policy.

TASK 2: Legal Analysis and Statutory Drafting.

Assume now that you are the lawyer for the federal government. At a meeting with congressional staffers interested in the lawsuit brought by Kansas, you are asked about the likelihood that the states's suit will succeed and what amendments to the law would make that result less likely.

a. Draft a memo analyzing the likelihood that a court would find the law to exceed Congress's powers under the Spending Clause.

b. Regardless of the conclusion you reach in that memo, redraft the statute in a way that maintains as much of its underlying policy as possible while reducing the chance that a court would find it unconstitutional.

Chapter 3

THE FEDERAL INTERSTATE COMMERCE POWER AND THE TENTH AMENDMENT

INTRODUCTION

This chapter considers Congress's Article I power to regulate "Commerce . . . among the several States." Article I, § 8, cl. 3. It also considers Tenth-Amendment-based limits on that power.

The Interstate Commerce Power

The Commerce Clause has been the subject of much debate and disagreement among Supreme Court justices. The following discussion provides only the most basic history, followed by a brief outline of the modern doctrinal rules.

Probably the first great opinion interpreting the Commerce Clause was *Gibbons v. Ogden*, 22 U.S. 1 (1824). Among other issues, *Gibbons* considered whether the Interstate Commerce Clause authorized Congress to regulate the ability of ships to navigate up and down the east coast of the United States. Chief Justice Marshall gave an expansive definition to the terms "commerce," to include navigation. *See Gibbons*, 22 U.S. at 193. Even more importantly, he gave a similarly expansive reading to the term "among the several States." He read that term to exclude only "the exclusively internal commerce of a State." *Gibbons*, 22 U.S. at 195. Immediately after writing that phrase, he continued:

> "The genius and character of the whole government seem to be, that its action is to be applied to all the external concerns of the nation, and to those internal concerns which affect the States generally; but not to those which are completely within a particular State, which do not affect other States, and with which it is not necessary to interfere, for the purpose of executing some of the general powers of the government. The completely internal commerce of a State, then, may be considered as reserved for the State itself." *Ibid.*

Later in the Nineteenth Century, and continuing into the first several decades of the Twentieth, the Court began to find limits on the commerce power. These limits were prompted by the increasing industrialization of the nation and the rise of calls for more aggressive federal regulation of what was quickly becoming a unified national economy. During this period, the Court held that Congress could not regulate activities whose impact on interstate commerce was only indirect, or activities, such as mining, manufacturing and agriculture, that were thought to be reserved for state regulation. *See, e.g., United States v. E.C. Knight Co.*, 156 U.S. 1 (1895) (federal power does not extend to regulation of manufacturing); *Carter v. Carter Coal Co.*, 298 U.S. 238 (1936) (federal power does not extend to regulation of activities that affect interstate commerce only indirectly).

This line of cases began to be questioned in *National Labor Relations Board v. Jones & Laughlin Steel Corp.*, 301 U.S. 1 (1937), where the Court concluded that federal regulation of the manufacturing activity of a large, integrated steel producer was constitutional, given the direct effects that activity had on interstate commerce. Later cases, in particular *United States v. Darby*, 312 U.S. 100 (1941) and *Wickard v. Filburn*, 317 U.S. 111 (1942) made explicit a new doctrine in which Congress had the power to regulate even local activities such as manufacturing, as long as Congress had a rational basis for believing that, in the aggregate, the regulated intrastate activity substantially affected interstate commerce.

The next major doctrinal development occurred in 1995, when the Court for the first time since 1936 struck down a federal law as exceeding the commerce power. *United States v. Lopez*, 514 U.S. 549 (1995). *Lopez* struck down a federal law making it a crime to bring a gun into a school zone. In *Lopez* the Court explained the three categories of federal power under the Commerce Clause.

First, Congress can regulate the channels of interstate commerce, *i.e*, the activities, such as buying and selling, that constitute interstate commerce. Second, it can regulate the instrumentalities of interstate commerce, i.e., the conduits through which interstate commerce passes (such as roads and railways). Finally, and most broadly, Congress can regulate activities that, while not themselves interstate commerce, substantially affect that commerce. The "substantial effects" prongs is the most heavily-debated aspect of Congress's power, as it allows Congress to regulate otherwise local activity, such as waste-dumping, paying school tuition or possessing controlled substances, as long as that activity satisfies the substantial effects test.

The modern doctrine provides two methods by which such local activity can be regulated under the "substantial effects" prong. First, if that activity is economic, then Congress can regulate it as long as (as stated in *Wickard*), it has a rational basis for believing that, in the aggregate, that activity substantially affects interstate commerce. Thus, in *Gonzales v. Raich*, 545 U.S. 1 (2005), the Court, consulting a dictionary, concluded that "possession" of marijuana constituted economic activity, and thus upheld federal penalties for drug possession, on the ground that Congress had a rational basis for believing that possession of a drug increased the risk of illicit interstate trafficking in that drug.

Second, if the activity is not economic then Congress can still regulate it if that regulation is an essential part of a broader regulatory scheme of economic activity. The Court also used this reasoning in *Raich*, observing that the federal drug possession ban was part of a comprehensive scheme regulating the manufacture, sale and purchase of drugs.

The *Lopez* Court suggested that in a doubtful case it might be helpful if Congress provided fact-findings noting the connection between the regulated activity and interstate commerce. *See* 549 U.S. at 563. However, five years later in *United States v. Morrison* the Court downplayed the importance of such findings when they supported the constitutionality of a statute that threatened "to completely obliterate the Constitution's distinction between national and local authority." 529 U.S. 598, 615 (2000).

The 2012 case upholding the constitutionality of the federal health care law, *National Federation of Independent Business v. Sebelius*, 183 L. Ed. 2d 450 (2012), added important new principles to the federal Commerce Clause power. In *dicta*, five justices would have struck down the federal healthcare law, otherwise known as the "Affordable Care Act" or "ACA," on the ground that it exceeded Congress's powers to regulate interstate commerce. These justices grounded their analysis on their conclusion that the statute regulated inactivity — that is, the status of not having insurance — by requiring such persons to purchase insurance. According to these justices, the Commerce Clause gives Congress the power to "regulate" "commerce," terms which imply the pre-existence of commercial activity.

Tenth Amendment Limits

For the last half-century the Supreme Court has debated whether Congress's Commerce Clause power is limited by the federalism implications of the Tenth Amendment. In *Maryland v. Wirtz*, 392 U.S. 183 (1968), the Court upheld extension of federal minimum wage law to a large class of state government employees. Eight years later, in *National League of Cities v. Usery*, 426 U.S. 833 (1976), the Court overruled *Wirtz* and held that the Commerce Clause did not authorize Congress to regulate state activity when that regulation "directly displace[s] the States' freedom to structure integral operations in areas of traditional governmental functions." *National League*, 426 U.S. at 852. Nine years later, the Court in turn overruled *National League of Cities*, holding that the Commerce Clause gave Congress the power to regulate the states as economic actors — e.g., as employers. *See Garcia v. San Antonio Metro. Trans. Authority*, 469 U.S. 528 (1985). Thus, when Congress is regulating interstate commerce general regulations may be imposed on states as well as private firms.

Since *Garcia*, however, the Court has recognized other Tenth Amendment-based limits on Congress's Commerce Clause authority. In *New York v. United States*, 505 U.S. 144 (1992), the Court held that Congress could not "commandeer" state governments, by requiring, as a matter of federal law, that states regulate in particular areas. The holding in *New York* was extended in *Printz v. United States*, 521 U.S. 898 (1997), to prohibit federal commandeering of state law enforcement, e.g., as in *Printz*, through a federal law requiring state law enforcement to make certain investigations. *Printz* stated, however, that the commandeering rule did not apply to state courts. In other words, even after *Printz* the federal government can "commandeer" state courts by requiring those courts to hear federal causes of action. *See Printz*, 521 U.S. at 929–930 (citing *Testa v. Katt*, 330 U.S. 386 (1947) (upholding a federal law requiring state courts to hear claims under that law).

Despite these limits, the anti-commandeering doctrine continues to allow Congress to work closely with states on regulatory goals, as long as it does not commandeer them. *New York* explicitly notes that Congress can regulate any area that comes within its Commerce Clause authority, and then give the states the option to do the actual implementation of the regulation, as long as states may opt out of participation (in which case a federal agency would take over). This is known as "cooperative federalism." Moreover, Congress may use its Spending Clause authority to induce states to regulate in particular ways, as long as such inducements are constitutional. *See* Chapter 2 (explaining limits on the spending power). Indeed, Congress can simply impose direct federal regulation, by-passing state authorities entirely.

Finally, in *Alden v. Maine*, 527 U.S. 706 (1999), the Court considered state sovereign immunity from having to defend a federal law cause of action in its own courts. The Eleventh Amendment does not apply in such situations, as that Amendment concerns state immunity from lawsuits in *federal* courts. *See* Chapter 4. In *Alden*, however, the Court imported Eleventh Amendment principles to apply to non-consenting states in state court. *See Alden*, 527 U.S. at 755–757. Those principles are discussed in Chapter 4; you should review that chapter's discussion of state sovereign immunity before continuing.

EXERCISE 3.1: FEDERAL PROTECTION OF WETLANDS

SKILLS AND VALUES UTILIZED: Task 1: Legal Writing and Editing. Task 2: Collaborative Writing.

PARTICIPANTS NEEDED: Task 1 can be performed individually. Task 2 must be done in teams of at least 2, and preferably 3 or 4.

ESTIMATED TIME FOR COMPLETION: 1 hour

LEVEL OF DIFFICULTY (1 to 5):

ROLE IN EXERCISE: Task 1: Editor and Writer of a Legal Memo. Task 2: Participant in Collaborative Writing.

TASKS: Task 1: Editing and drafting a legal memo. Task 2: Working collaboratively to combine individual work into a single product.

Last month, Congress enacted the Wetlands Protection Act (WPA). The WPA reads as follows:

Section 1: Findings

The Congress hereby finds the following:

(1)   Wetlands and wetland-adjacent areas are important breeding and stop-off points for various types of migratory birds;

(2)   Wetlands and wetland-adjacent areas are being lost to residential and business park development at alarming rates.

Section 2: Prohibition on Development

(a)   No large-scale development shall be constructed on any wetland or wetland-adjacent area if the United States Army Corps of Engineers determines that the land at issue is critical habitat for migratory birds and that mitigation measures would not adequately protect the species.

(b)   "Large-scale development" means any development encompassing more than 1,000 acres.

You and your colleagues are second-year associates at a firm that represents the National Association of Home Builders. The partner in charge of that client has asked a summer associate to draft a short memo analyzing the constitutionality of the WPA under the Interstate Commerce Clause. The pertinent part of the memo is provided below. The partner calls you and your colleagues in and gives you two tasks.

TASK 1: *Editing and Legal Drafting.* You and your colleagues are asked to identify the structural and substantive flaws of the memo and then rewrite it. She asks you to do this individually. The point of this assignment is both to provide training to the summer associate who wrote the first draft, and to prepare for Task 2, below.

TASK 2: *Collaborative Writing.* You and your colleagues are asked to share both your assessment of the original memo and your revised memos with the rest of the group, and together to draft a memo that will be presented to the client.

MEMO

From: Summer Associate

To: Peter Jackson

Date: [date]

Subject: Constitutionality of the Wetlands Protection Act (WPA)

Question Presented

You asked me to analyze the constitutionality of the WPA under the Interstate Commerce Clause . . . .

Analysis

In sum the statute is probably constitutional. The statute has findings, which may help but maybe not depending on the subject-matter. One way to analyze the issue is that migratory birds substantially affect the instrumentalities of interstate commerce. The basic question is whether the statute comes within the Interstate Commerce Power. It also regulates the activity of building, which helps.

The Court would likely be deferential here because this is clearly impacting interstate commerce so you could do aggregation. Building large-scale real estate developments is clearly an economic activity so that probably means the statute survives. To be constitutional, the statute either has to regulate the channels or the instrumentalities of interstate commerce, or an activity that substantially affects it. The problem is that the statute seems to aim at environmental conservation, which is not what the interstate commerce power was intended to protect. Another problem is that land use is something that has traditionally been regulated by states.*

---

* Note to students: You can assume the factual correctness of this statement.

EXERCISE 3.2: INVOLVING THE STATES IN A FEDERAL PROGRAM

SKILLS AND VALUES UTILIZED:

- Legal Analysis
- Legal Writing
- Collaboration
- Statutory Drafting

PARTICIPANTS NEEDED: This task should be performed in groups of 2–4.

ESTIMATED TIME FOR COMPLETION: 1 hour

LEVEL OF DIFFICULTY (1 to 5):

ROLE IN EXERCISE: Attorney assisting in legislative drafting.

TASK: Drafting.

After completing the tasks above, the partner invites you and your colleagues into a meeting with the client, the National Association of Home Builders. The client explains that its members would prefer that the "critical habitat" and mitigation decisions referred to in the statute be made by state environmental authorities, rather than by the federal government. But he also recognizes that Congress is going to continue insisting on certain minimum federal standards for habitat protection. Thus, he would like that law to be amended so as to make room for state regulation within the context of a federal regulatory regime. The client remembers vaguely that there are some Tenth Amendment limits on Congress's ability to require states to take particular actions. But he also remembers that there are ways around those limits. He also explains that he has set up a meeting with a friendly congressman, and that he would like to have in hand some statutory language that would amend the WPA in a way that accomplishes his objective but also is constitutional.

TASK 3: Draft statutory language amending the WPA so as to make states responsible for the critical habitat and mitigation decisions, without running afoul of the Tenth Amendment.

Chapter 4

STATE SOVEREIGN IMMUNITY AND CONGRESSIONAL POWER TO ENFORCE THE FOURTEENTH AMENDMENT

INTRODUCTION

This chapter's problem will test your knowledge of several different doctrinal areas: Congress's power to regulate interstate commerce, the states' Eleventh Amendment sovereign immunity, and Congress's power to enforce the Fourteenth Amendment. The first of these areas has already been covered in Chapter 3. You should review that discussion before starting this problem.

State Sovereign Immunity:

The Eleventh Amendment states as follow: "The Judicial power of the United States shall not be construed to extend to any suit in law or equity, commenced or prosecuted against one of the United States by Citizens of another State, or by Citizens or Subjects of any Foreign State." While the text of this Amendment seemingly does not apply to a suit by a citizen of a state against her own state, that interpretation was rejected by the Court in *Hans v. Louisiana*, 134 U.S. 1 (1890), which concluded that the Amendment reaffirmed traditional state sovereign immunity, including a state's immunity from suit against its own citizens. The Amendment does not apply to suits brought in *state* court; however, the Supreme Court in *Alden v. Maine*, 527 U.S. 706 (1999) imported Eleventh Amendment principles to apply, via the Tenth Amendment, to cases brought in state courts. See Chapter 3 for a discussion of this principle.

Eleventh Amendment immunity is not absolute. For example, states can voluntarily waive their sovereign immunity, as long as they do so clearly and unambiguously. Beyond such waiver, the two most common ways of overcoming it are through the *Ex parte Young* doctrine, and congressional abrogation of state sovereign immunity.

Young: Under the doctrine of *Ex parte Young*, 209 U.S. 123 (1908), a plaintiff can overcome state sovereign immunity by suing a state official, rather than the state itself. The theory is that a state official is powerless to violate federal law; thus, when a plaintiff alleges such a violation, the official-defendant is "stripped" of his cloak of state immunity. *Young* suits are subject to significant limitations, however. Aside from the requirement that the plaintiff sue the officer, not the state itself, the suit must seek prospective relief (e.g., an injunction) rather than retrospective relief (e.g., damages). *Edelman v. Jordan*, 415 U.S. 651 (1974). Even if the requested relief is styled as prospective, it may not be allowed if as a practical matter it is indistinguishable from relief against the state itself. *Coeur d'Alene Tribe v. Idaho*, 521 U.S. 261 (1997). The claim must be based on violations of federal, not state, law. *Pennhurst State School & Hosp. v. Halderman*, 465 U.S. 89 (1984). Finally, if Congress enacts a statute that includes within it a "detailed remedial scheme" then that choice by Congress is held to supersede and thus preclude the availability of relief under *Young*. *Seminole Tribe v. Florida*, 517 U.S. 44 (1996). (Note that such a detailed remedial scheme may itself not be available, if it was not enacted pursuant to a grant of power that authorizes Congress to abrogate state sovereign immunity. See the next paragraph for more information on which grants of power authorize Congress to abrogate states' immunity.)

Abrogation: States' immunity can also be overcome if Congress enacts a statute abrogating states' sovereign immunity. Such abrogation statements must be clear and unambiguous. *See, e.g., Pennsylvania v. Union Gas*, 491 U.S. 1 (1989) (discussing whether a particular statute included such a clear abrogation statement). Additionally, not all of Congress's legislative powers authorize it to abrogate state sovereign immunity. Most notably, Congress's Article I power to regulate interstate commerce has been held not to authorize it to abrogate state immunity. *See Seminole Tribe, supra*. However, Congress does have the power to abrogate state sovereign immunity when it legislates pursuant to its power to enforce the Fourteenth Amendment. *See Fitzpatrick v. Bitzer*, 427 U.S. 445 (1976).

Congressional Power to Enforce the Fourteenth Amendment:

Section 5 of the Fourteenth Amendment authorizes Congress "to enforce, by appropriate legislation, the provisions" of the rest of the Amendment. (Very similarly-worded provisions appear in the Thirteenth, Fifteenth, Nineteenth, Twenty-Third, Twenty-Fourth, and Twenty-Sixth Amendments.) One of the first Supreme Court statements about the meaning of "the Section 5 Power" was in *The Civil Rights Cases*, 109 U.S. 3 (1883). In that case the Court struck down the Civil Rights Act of 1875, which banned discrimination in public accommodations (e.g., restaurants and theaters) on the ground that Section 5 only gave Congress the authority to remedy conduct by states, rather than private parties.

After *The Civil Rights Cases* the Section 5 power fell into desuetude, as Reconstruction ended and Congress grew hostile to civil rights legislation. By the 1960s, however, Congress was again interested in protecting civil rights. The Interstate Commerce Clause provided the constitutional authority for some of these laws, such as the Civil Rights Act of 1964. Other laws, however, such as the Voting Rights Act of 1965, were grounded in either the Fourteenth or Fifteenth Amendment, both of which have Enforcement Clauses that are similarly worded and have been interpreted to provide the same amount of power. (The Fifteenth Amendment prohibits racial discrimination with regard to the right to vote.)

In *South Carolina v. Katzenbach*, 383 U.S. 301 (1966), the Court upheld provisions of the Voting Rights Act that had been attacked as exceeding Congress's power to enforce the Fifteenth Amendment. The Court concluded that Congress's power to enforce that Amendment (and, by implication, the Fourteenth) was as broad as

Congress's powers under the Necessary and Proper Clause, quoting Chief Justice Marshall's famous language about that latter provision: "Let the end be legitimate, let it be within the scope of the constitution, and all means which are appropriate, which are plainly adapted to that end, which are not prohibited, but consist with the letter and spirit of the constitution, are constitutional." *McCulloch v. Maryland*, 17 U.S. 316, 421 (1819).

Later in that same term, the Court decided *Katzenbach v. Morgan*, 384 U.S. 641 (1966). *Morgan* upheld another provision of the Voting Rights Act, that granted people the right to vote, even if they were not literate in English, as long as they had achieved a certain grade level in a Puerto Rican school. (This provision was aimed at ensuring the right to vote to the Puerto Rican community in New York.) The Court employed two theories in upholding this provision of the statute as appropriate legislation under the Fourteenth Amendment. First, the Court concluded that this law helped indirectly ensure equal treatment for the Puerto Rican community in New York, by providing them the political clout that would help ensure their equal treatment by state and local government. *See Morgan*, 384 U.S. at 652-653. Second, and more controversially, it suggested that Congress could have reasonably concluded that deprivation of voting rights to this community *directly* violated the Equal Protection Clause. *See Morgan*, 384 U.S. at 653-656.

The second of these interpretations of the Section 5 power was squarely rejected thirty years later, in *City of Boerne v. Flores*, 521 U.S. 507 (1997). *Boerne* held that the second *Morgan* theory would allow Congress to step over the line from "enforcing" to "interpreting" the Fourteenth Amendment, the latter of which was a function reserved to the Supreme Court. The Court instead required that Section 5 legislation be "congruent and proportional" to the constitutional violations the legislation sought to remedy or deter. *See City of Boerne*, 521 U.S. at 530. Applying this standard, it struck down the Religious Freedom Restoration Act, a law that imposed greater restrictions on state laws that burdened religious exercise than what Free Exercise doctrine imposed. (This right was incorporated into the Fourteenth Amendment via the Due Process Clause, and thus within Congress's Fourteenth Amendment enforcement power.) The Court reasoned that there was insufficient evidence that states were violating the First Amendment right of free religious exercise. '

In cases after *Boerne* the Court has refined its approach to the congruence and proportionality analysis. Ultimately, the Court has explained the test as a three-step analysis. First, the Court must "identify with some precision the scope of the constitutional right at issue." *Board of Trustees v. Garrett*, 531 U.S. 356, 365 (2001). Second, the Court must "examine whether Congress identified a history and pattern" of unconstitutional conduct regarding that right. *Garrett*, 531 U.S. at 368. Finally, the Court must consider whether the statute imposes burdens on the states that are out of proportion to the record of violations. *See, e.g., Kimel v. Board of Regents*, 528 U.S. 62, 88-89 (2000) (concluding that Congress had assembled an insufficient record of unconstitutional state government age discrimination to justify the broad burdens imposed by the Age Discrimination in Employment Act); *Tennessee v. Lane*, 541 U.S. 509, 532-533 (2004) (concluding that the public accommodations provisions of the ADA, as applied to access to courthouses, closely tracked the constitutional requirements for access to the judicial process).

An important aspect of the Court's Section 5 jurisprudence is that the significance of the constitutional right protected by the Section 5 legislation matters a great deal in the congruence and proportionality analysis. For example, in *Garrett* the Court insisted on a very strong evidentiary showing in the Americans With Disabilities Act, the statute at issue in that case, largely because the discrimination the statute targeted — disability discrimination — was subject only to rational basis review. Conversely, in *Nevada Dept of Human Resources v. Hibbs*, 538 U.S. 721 (2003), the Court upheld the Family and Medical Leave Act (FMLA) as appropriate legislation enforcing the equal protection right of gender equality. The *Hibbs* Court noted that gender was a quasi-suspect classification in equal protection law, and concluded that that fact made it easier for Congress to demonstrate a factual record justifying the legislation: "Because the standard for demonstrating the constitutionality of a gender-based classification is more difficult to meet than our rational-basis test . . . it was easier for Congress to show a pattern of state constitutional violations" in the FMLA, as compared with the ADA in *Garrett. Id.* at 736. However, the Court must be convinced that the enforcement provision was in fact targeted at the discrimination. *See Coleman v. Court of Appeals*, 182 L.Ed.2d 296 (2012) (striking down, as exceeding Congress's enforcement power, the "self-care" provision of the FMLA, on the ground that it did not combat sex discrimination in the workplace).

EXERCISE 4.1: GENETICS DISCRIMINATION

SKILLS AND VALUES UTILIZED:

- Legal Analysis

- Identifying Legally-Relevant Facts

GENERAL DESCRIPTION OF EXERCISE: Task 1: Drafting a memo analyzing the constitutional issues relevant to your client's claim. Task 2: identifying the facts relevant to those constitutional issues.

PARTICIPANTS NEEDED: This task is best performed in groups of 2–4.

ESTIMATED TIME FOR COMPLETION: 2 hours

LEVEL OF DIFFICULTY (1 to 5):

ROLE IN EXERCISE: Attorney for a client considering litigation.

In the summer after your second year of law school you are interning at a firm that does employment discrimination law. Rhonda Rainmaker, your supervisor, comes into your office and says the following:

"I just talked to a guy named Paul Plunkett. Paul is a tool maker for the New Jersey Department of Transportation. I should say 'was a tool maker'; three months ago he was fired. And, get this, he was fired for having bad genes! His boss told Paul that some routine medical testing the company did on him revealed a genetic predisposition for sudden arthritic outbreak (SAO). I had to look that up — it turns out SAO is a disease where you get a sudden temporary hardening of muscles that makes them hard to move. The boss said that put him at risk for workplace injuries, so they fired him, even though he has never had an SAO incident in his life. I took some notes from the interview I had with him; they're attached to this packet.

"Based on what Paul told me it seems clear that his employer violated that new federal law dealing with genetic discrimination in employment, 'GINA' I think it's called. This is a fairly new law so the constitutional issues haven't been resolved. I can work on the question whether the employer violated the statute, but I need you to work on the constitutional law angle.

"Like I said, don't worry about whether Paul has a good claim under the statute, you can assume that. You can also assume that the statute authorizes the type of relief Paul wants (which is explained in the interview notes, below). What I need from you is to figure out if there any constitutional issues stopping Paul from getting the relief he wants.

"Second, we also need to figure out what information we need to address the constitutional law issues you've identified. The paralegals have assembled the attached set of documents, which they've identified as Appendices A-D. Take a look at those documents and identify the information relevant to our issues. Put each piece of information you find in a table, and note the issue for which it's relevant, and explain why and in which direction it cuts. The paralegals have prepared the template of the table for you, at the end of this packet.

"Remember — the New Jersey Department of Transportation is an arm of the state; it's not a subdivision like a county or a city. That means we might have sovereign immunity issues. I don't know if it helps, but if it does, you can assume that New Jersey didn't waive its sovereign immunity; they never do that over there."

TASK 1: *Legal Analysis and Drafting:* Outline a memo that explains, in logical form, the constitutional law issues that would likely arise from Paul's claim for relief.

TASK 2: *Fact Identification:* Using all the information provided in the appendices below, create the table described above.

Note: It will be helpful if you perform these tasks at the same time. In particular, as you consider the Constitutional Law issues as part of your performance of Task 1, you will encounter factual questions that you should acknowledge as part of your performance of Task 2.

APPENDIX A
"The Genetic Information Non-Discrimination Act of 2010"

<u>Section 1:</u> <u>Findings:</u> The Congress hereby finds that:

A. Workplace discrimination based on a person's genetic make-up costs the American economy billions of dollars every year.

B. The role of genetics in diseases is still largely unknown. Unfortunately, too many Americans treat genetics as a clear cause of many diseases.

C. Discrimination based on genetics is generally inappropriate given the inability of humans to alter their genetic make-up. Indeed, one's genes are perhaps the most truly immutable characteristics a human possesses.

D. In the past Americans have suffered significant discrimination because of their genetic make-up. Moreover, the fear and shame that often accompanies disclosure of a genetic predisposition to a disease often leads Americans to hide their conditions. In this sense, Americans with such predispositions truly constitute a discrete and insular minority.

<u>Section 2:</u> <u>Authority</u>

Congress enacts this law pursuant to its power to regulate Interstate Commerce. To the extent the statute regulates states, Congress acts under both the Interstate Commerce Power and its power to enforce the Equal Protection Clause.

<u>Section 3:</u> <u>Discrimination Prohibited:</u>

A. No employer shall discriminate against an employee based on that employee's genetic make-up.

B. Nothing in this law prohibits an employer from taking actions to ensure the safety of the workplace when an employee manifests an actual medical condition that threatens the health and safety of the employee or any other person.

<u>Section 4:</u> <u>Remedies</u>

Employees subject to discrimination based on their genetic make-up may sue their employers in federal court in the district where the discrimination took place, for any relief the court deems appropriate.

<u>Section 5:</u> <u>Definitions</u>

. . . (5) "Employer" means any person who employs another person, and includes any state or subdivision thereof.

APPENDIX B

An excerpt from Tabitha Tenurehappy, *The New Frontier of Anti-Discrimination Law: Genetic Discrimination*, 54 STATE U. LAW REVIEW 657, 669–672 (2007)

[NOTE: YOU CAN ASSUME THAT THE FACTUAL STATEMENTS MADE IN THIS FICTITIOUS LAW REVIEW ARTICLE ARE TRUE.]

History

. . . The history books are full of examples of horrific discrimination imposed on people with actual or perceived genetic predispositions for diseases or other medical conditions. By the late nineteenth century it had become clear that certain diseases and conditions were passed from one generation to another. This led states to impose severe discrimination against people who were thought to have "defective genes." For example, states often banned such individuals from getting married. If such a woman nevertheless became pregnant, the law often forced her to undergo an abortion, in order, as one Indiana law of this type stated, "to prevent the decline of the human race into degradation and disease."

The science of the time was not sufficiently advanced to do accurate genetic testing; thus, attempts to regulate based on genetics often led to grotesquely overbroad legislation. For example, persons with predispositions to one disease were thought to have generally defective genes, which made them weaker overall. In addition, popular fears grew that genetic predispositions explained far more than the limited set of medical conditions that scientists thought were genetically based. Thus, the presence of an inherited condition, or even being the relative of someone with such a condition, often triggered social shunning and legal restrictions, based on the fear that a person with one predisposition likely possessed other weaknesses, and were fundamentally defective humans. This dynamic often triggered cascading discrimination, where a distant relative's possession of a disease that might be inherited created a series of discriminatory exclusions. In addition to the marriage and procreation discrimination described above, such exclusions also included denials of university admission, on the ground that the applicant was "mentally defective," exclusions from the professions (such as law, medicine and teaching), on the ground that such persons were at risk for immorality and incompetence, and denials to immigrants of the right to apply for American citizenship, given concern that they would become burdens on society.

Modern Discrimination, and the Legal Response

Modern society continues to witness the types of discrimination noted above, though thankfully in smaller amounts. The legal response has been disappointing, though not uniformly so. Courts have usually dismissed most genetic discrimination claims as simply not violating any law. (Claims under disability law exist only when the discrimination is based on the actual disease or condition, not a genetic predisposition toward the disease.) While a federal genetics discrimination act is advancing in Congress, advocacy efforts remain hobbled by the fact that there remains a stigma to possessing certain genetic markers. Ironically, this stigma has caused many persons to keep their genetic status a secret, thus impeding group advocacy. On the other hand, legislators have noted that genetics discrimination is more or less randomly distributed in the population. This fact has led some scholars to speculate that legislators might not feel as much pressure to oppose anti-discrimination legislation of this sort, since, as one legislator explained in sponsoring a bill, "this kind of discrimination could happen to anyone."

When the discriminator has been a governmental body, plaintiffs have raised equal protection claims. These claims have also usually failed. In the approximately 50 lawsuits alleging unconstitutional genetics-based discrimination since 1980, 45 were dismissed after the judge, usually performing very deferential review, found a rational basis for the discrimination. Most of the reported appellate opinions gave at least some thought to whether genetics ought to be a suspect class, given that neither the Supreme Court nor any federal appellate court has considered the equal protection status of genetic make-ups. These opinions all rejected heightened scrutiny, often after expressing concern that heightened scrutiny would embroil courts in difficult medical and bio-ethical questions.

Of the five remaining lawsuits, two were decided for the plaintiff based on the existence of evidence that the government actor had a subjective dislike of the plaintiff based on the plaintiff's genetic make-up. A third suit was resolved for the plaintiff after the court applied what it called "rational basis plus" scrutiny, a standard it applied after concluding that the immutability of genetic make-ups rendered genetics discrimination "constitutionally at least a bit suspicious." In the final two suits the parties settled before trial . . . .

APPENDIX C
Report of the Task Force on Genetics and American Life, Delivered to Congress December 27, 2007

[NOTE: YOU CAN ASSUME THAT THE FACTUAL STATEMENTS MADE IN THIS FICTITIOUS REPORT ARE TRUE.]

I. Introduction

The Task Force is pleased to present its findings to Congress as it considers the problem of genetic discrimination . . . .

I. Findings

1. *Discrimination based on genetic make-up occurs frequently in American life.* We have observed a wide variety of organizations excluding persons known to have genetic predispositions to diseases. As is well known, insurers often reject applications for insurance based on such predispositions. In addition, employers have refused to give more challenging (and thus higher status) job assignments to such persons, based on the fear that "they might get sick." We have also heard reports of employees being fired, and applicants being rejected for jobs, based on this same rationale. Sports teams of all types, from professional teams to Little League baseball, have excluded would-be members for the same reason. Universities, churches, and other civic organizations have also excluded such persons, often based on the fear that a genetic predisposition to one disease somehow makes that person more prone to other conditions that either would harm their other members or otherwise make that individual less desirable as a member.

2. *Much of this discrimination is unwarranted.* We recognize that genetic predispositions to diseases are relevant to a variety of life situations. However, much of the discrimination the Task Force uncovered reflects mistaken judgments that persons with such predispositions are inherently less worthy. Frankly, task force members were shocked at the virulence of the public's attitudes toward people with such predispositions. Words like "dirty," "defective," "dangerous" and even "sub-human" were heard not infrequently in our interviews. Such attitudes have led many Americans to refrain from disclosing their genetic information, or even joining organizations dedicated to working on these issues.

3. *Much of this discrimination is problematic because of the lack of an individual's control over his or her genes.* The Task Force believes that the basic promise of America — that one should be judged based on one's conduct, rather than based on factors beyond one's control — requires that genetic discrimination be tightly limited to situations where genetics are obviously relevant. Indeed, even in such limited circumstances genetic discrimination may be justifiably prohibited, in order to provide a full measure of human dignity to all.

4.   *Stamping out genetic discrimination need not be overly burdensome.* Without delving into fine legal distinctions about how much genetic discrimination, if any, should be allowed, the common-sense fact is that much genetic discrimination could be avoided if Americans were willing to make slight accommodations and bear small inconveniences and expense. For example, Americans could be asked to pay slightly higher health insurance premiums, in order for those with genetic predispositions to have access to insurance. Employers might be forced to bear slightly higher costs to transfer someone with a genetic predisposition out of a job that is hazardous for him only when the predisposition manifests itself into an actual disease, rather than simply refusing to hire that person to begin with. Most of all, Americans could learn about genetics, which would likely change many of their current negative attitudes.

Respectfully submitted,

Rodrigo Dominguez, MD, Chair, Disabilities Policy Committee of the American Medical Association

Susan Helford, Professor of Law, Rogers State University School of Law, New Hope City, Hew Hope

Samuel Bergland, Chair, Policy Committee of the Association of Disabled Americans

APPENDIX D
Notes of Interview with Paul Plunkett

- Pltf was an employee for the N.J. Dept of Trans. Got good performance evals — "never missed a day of work in seven years."

- Genetics show he is susceptible to "sudden arthritic outbreak" (SAO). Never had an incidence of it. Passed on from mother's side of family.

- Employer found out, and pltf was immediately fired. Supervisor: "we can't take a chance on your hands freezing up while you're working on the equipment." No advance notice at all! Employer found out Thursday morning and fired pltf Friday afternoon.

- Out of work for three months. Situation got tough, nearly ran out of money. Found job with Smith Industries last week, very happy with job. Doesn't want to go back to the old job, but wants damages and back pay for the three months of lost wages. Also wants an injunction "so they can't do this to other people like me."

FACT TABLE

Fact	Issue to Which It is Relevant	Why Relevant? Which Side Does it Favor?

Chapter 5

FEDERAL EXECUTIVE POWERS

INTRODUCTION

The Constitution states, "the executive Power shall be vested in a President." Article II. Thus, the powers allotted to the executive branch in Article II are not divided among positions or people, but instead are entrusted to a single person, the president.

It long has been established that the executive's powers extend beyond the express grant of powers in the Constitution to include implied and inherent powers as well. The scope of both express and implied powers has been tested over the years by the foundational principle of the separation of powers, which limits the three branches from usurping powers of the other branches. Courts often must decide whether an apparent encroachment by one branch of government on the power of another is constitutionally permissible. In addition, sometimes the federal government encroaches on powers committed to states, raising intergovernmental issues falling under the heading of federalism.

A. THE PRESIDENT'S APPOINTMENT AND REMOVAL POWERS

The powers of the three branches of government are generally non-transferable, whether the power is given away or usurped. The unconstitutionality of a branch giving away its own powers is called the nondelegation of powers doctrine. *See generally Buckley v. Valeo*, 424 U.S. 936 (1976).

These principles govern the ability of a branch of government to appoint or remove government officials in an area of power that is really a subsidiary of the separation of powers doctrine. While appointment and removal of federal officers have been the focus of numerous cases, there is only an explicit provision relating to appointments, and not removal. The Appointments Clause states that "the Congress may by Law vest the Appointment of such inferior Officers, as they think proper, in the President alone, in the courts of Law, or in the Heads of Departments." This clause effectively divides appointments of officials into two categories — those persons considered an officer of the United States and those persons who are "inferior officers." The definition of officers is saddled with some ambiguity. Based on Supreme Court pronouncements, primary officers generally report directly to the President without an intervening superior who directs and supervises the other's work. *See Edmond v. United States*, 520 U.S. 651, 661 (1997). By comparison, inferior officers can be removed by a superior executive official and have limits associated with their jurisdiction, tenure, and duties. *See Morrison v. Olson*, 487 U.S. 654, 671-672 (1988).

The permissible appointment procedure varies, depending on the type of official to be hired. The highest ranking officials, including ambassadors, federal judges, and the heads of departments, such as the Secretaries of State and Defense, are nominated by the president and then appointed, after the Senate provides its "advice and consent" (meaning approval). The appointment of the remaining officers, called "inferior officers" by the Constitution (although these positions are anything but "inferior"), reflects the interdependence of the branches of government. The Appointments Clause gives Congress the power to create the office, but not to appoint who fills it. Congress can play a role in determining who appoints an inferior officer, such as the president, heads of departments, or the judiciary. Thus, even inferior executive officials are not always appointed by the president, but must depend sometimes on other branches of government. In particular, Congress can choose to vest the power entirely in the president, the courts or the heads of departments. *See Buckley v. Valeo*, 424 U.S. 936 (1976), which illustrates that Congress' extensive powers to create offices and appoint officials have limits.

The president has an additional temporary appointment power that often is put to use. If a vacancy exists when the Senate is in recess, the president has the power to fill the vacancy under Article II, Section 2, Clause 3. These recess appointments, as they are known, last only until the end of the Senate's next term. While the appointments are only for a limited duration, the recess power has been used to give controversial nominees an on-the-job try-out. Starting with George Washington, presidents have used this clause to populate the federal judiciary with preferred judges and to fill other governmental positions. While most officials receiving recess appointments lose their jobs when their terms expire, some have been subsequently confirmed through the regular appointments process. One such successful recess appointee included the former lead counsel for the NAACP and future Supreme Court justice, Thurgood Marshall, who had been appointed to the Second Circuit Court of Appeals.

While the hiring or appointments power is outlined in the Constitution, the document is silent on whether and how the president can fire or remove officers who have assumed their positions. With respect to Article III judges, who hold their positions for life as long as they demonstrate good behavior, the removal process is eminently clear: only impeachment will suffice for removal. For other officials, it seems almost tautological that if the president has the power to appoint, the power to remove should follow, especially for officers exercising an executive function. This deductive reasoning process, however, is not completely accurate, and the Supreme Court has fashioned a jurisprudence of shared responsibility between the president and Congress for the removal of officers.

Given the predominance of interconnected powers, the executive's power to remove officials extends to officials operating at least partially outside of the executive branch. These officials are not purely executive officers, but can be considered hybrid officials. For example, an official in the Federal Trade Commission might have some judicial duties. With hybrid appointees, the president's removal powers are diminished. Attempts to unilaterally fire the official may be improper, and Congress can create job descriptions that include the length of the hybrid officials' terms and the bases for removal. Even if Congress has not specified how a hybrid official can be removed, principles of separation of powers, and one of its derivatives, autonomy of action, have created a barrier to executive interference. *See Wiener v. United States.* 357 U.S. 349 (1958).

There are other dimensions of the removal doctrine. If the legislature authorizes hiring an officer with an executive function, the legislature also cannot wield broad removal power with respect to that officer. For example, in *Bowsher v. Synar*, 478 U.S. 714 (1986), the Congress passed the Balanced Budget and Emergency Deficit Act of 1985 to try to reduce the federal deficit. The act authorized the Comptroller General to determine the appropriate budget cuts and to relay that information to the president for implementation. The law permitted the removal of the Comptroller General based on a number of grounds, including "inefficiency," or "malfeasance." In finding this removal scheme unconstitutional, the Court held that the legislature violated the separation of powers doctrine by creating a position within the executive sphere and then reserving its own authority to remove an official charged with executing the law.

In *Morrison v. Olson*, 487 U.S. 654 (1988), however, the Supreme Court upheld a law limiting the president's removal of an independent counsel only for good cause, as distinguished from removal at the will of the president. This holding is consonant with the view that even some inferior officers who have an executive function might not always be subject to removal by the president alone.

In *Free Enterprise Fund v. Public Co. Accounting Bd.*, 130 S. Ct. 3138 (2010), the Supreme Court considered whether a multilevel removal scheme was constitutional. The case involved certain aspects of the Public Company Accounting Oversight Board, as created pursuant to the Sarbanes-Oxley Act. The Board was intended to provide greater oversight on the auditing process of public companies. Pursuant to the Sarbanes Oxley Act, the Securities and Exchange Commission (SEC) would be responsible for appointing members to the Oversight Board. In addition, the Board members only could be removed for cause by the Commissioners, not by the President. The Commissioners also could be removed only for cause. Thus, the President did not have direct removal power over the Board members, only a form of appellate or secondary review of the propriety of the Commissioners' actions.

The Court was presented with the question of whether Congress could create such a removal scheme. In *Free Enterprise Fund*, the Court decided that the combinatory effect of two removals for cause was unconstitutional. Chief Justice Roberts, writing for the Court, stated:

"We hold that such multilevel protection from removal is contrary to Article II's vesting of the executive power in the President. The President cannot 'take Care that the Laws be faithfully executed' if he cannot oversee the faithfulness of the officers who execute them. Here the President cannot remove an officer who enjoys more than one level of good-cause protection, even if the President determines that the officer is neglecting his duties or discharging them improperly." *Free Enterprise Fund*, at 3147.

EXERCISE 5.1: THE AMERICAN JOBS BANK

SKILLS AND VALUES UTILIZED:

- Drafting of laws

- Critical Analysis and Application

- Persuasive Advocacy

ESTIMATED TIME FOR COMPLETION: 1 hour

LEVEL OF DIFFICULTY (1 to 5):

ROLE IN EXERCISE: You are a staff attorney for freshman Senator Susan Marcus of North Dakota, who, after a solo sojourn to the North Pole, has an epiphany — a way to create thousands of American jobs, with no tax increase for 99% of Americans.

EXERCISE: Senator Marcus wishes to propose a bill creating a government company that would fund and foster jobs for Americans. The enterprise would operate as a capital support system for entrepreneurs, and be called the American Entrepreneur Job Bank. (AEJB). The AEJB also would assist in furthering the education of Americans for 21st Century jobs. The primary goal of the AEJB is to create more American-made products through American jobs, and keep those people with great ideas in the United States the place of origin for those ideas. To gain support for the bill, Marcus would partner with a member of the opposing party, Senator James.

A. Appointments

The Company is to be run by a Chief Executive Officer (CEO) and Chief Operating Officer (COO). The tenure of the CEO shall be indefinite and the COO shall be appointed for a ten-year period, with a potential renewal of two five-year periods. Senator James would like these appointments to be made by the Executive branch, with prior approval by a bipartisan committee of neutral business leaders comprised of the deans of the top-ten ranked business schools. Senator Marcus would like Congress to have some role in the appointments process, vetting potential candidates and limiting who is eligible for the positions. Senator Marcus also wants the government to have no say in the day-to-day operations of this company other than outlining goals for the AEJB. Senator James is willing to give total policy control to the CEO and board of advisors to the company. Both senators agree that the COO and the Chief Financial Officer should be approved by the CEO, but should be first approved for consideration by a Congressional subcommittee. The CEO would appoint or delegate the appointment of other company employees.

B. Removal of CEO and COO

Under the proposal, Senator Marcus recognizes that only the President should have the authority to remove the CEO and COO of the AEJB, but wants any removal to be at least for "legitimate business grounds," including, but not limited to, insubordination, neglect of responsibilities, and lack of productivity. (No exacting definition of "legitimate business grounds" would be provided). Even if the President legitimately removes the officer, Senator Marcus wants the removal to be in writing, even if the disassociation is temporary.

C. Removal of the CFO

Both senators agree that the CFO should be removed only by the CEO, and only on a "reasonable basis," meaning the basis is one that would likely lead to a similar dismissal in the private sector. While the basis need not reach the "just cause" level, there must be some reason provided by the CEO in writing that is neither arbitrary nor capricious.

TASK: Draft a revised law that overcomes constitutional challenges.

B.   THE PRESIDENT'S COMMANDER-IN-CHIEF POWERS

Article II, Section 2, Clause 1, states that the president is the "Commander-in-Chief of the Army and Navy of the United States." This statement offers the president not only a shared role in combating war and foreign aggression, but over time has given the president the upper hand in deploying the armed forces in national security matters. Many presidents have advanced the belief that the presidency possesses considerable implied powers, particularly in responding pragmatically with armed forces to national threats. The Supreme Court has corroborated the idea of at least some implied executive powers. *See, e.g., In re Neagle*, 135 U.S. 1 (1890). The rationale for this view is that since the Constitution does not formally reject implied and inherent powers and since the president is located as the figurative and literal leader of the country, the presidency has unstated powers at its disposal. Teddy Roosevelt, a proponent of this position, opined, "My belief was that it was not only [the president's] right but his duty to do anything that the needs of the Nation demanded unless such action was forbidden by the Constitution or laws." This view has been more prevalent in challenging times, particularly in the past decades with America playing a large peace-keeping role as well as fighting terrorism around the world. The decision to provide air assistance to NATO in protecting the rebels in Libya in 2011 is but a recent example of unilateral action taken by the executive branch.

The emergence of the executive as the primary decision maker in issues of national security, particularly in its powers over committing troops to armed conflict, led the Congress to reassert its shared constitutional role. In 1973, Congress passed the War Powers Resolution. Over the opposition of President Nixon and his veto, the Act attempted to frame the circumstances and length of time the president could commit troops abroad without consulting or seeking the approval of Congress. The Act imposed reporting requirements on the president if troops were deployed and limited the situations when troop deployments were permissible. Under the Act, the president could still deploy troops in certain circumstances, but only if there was a declaration of war, specific statutory authorization, or a national emergency resulting from an attack on the United States, its territories, or its armed forces. If deployment is authorized, the president must still report back to the Congress with the president's rationale. The president can maintain such an action unilaterally only for a limited amount of time, unless an extension is granted by Congress.

Since the enactment of the law, presidents have effectively skirted or ignored its mandate. With the rise of terroristic threats following the attacks of September 11, 2001, the executive branch has claimed increasing authority to act in an insular and secret manner, without consultation or approval. How the War Powers Resolution Act applies in this dynamic, uncertain and increasingly global environment is unclear.

1. The War Powers Resolution

Congress passed the War Powers Resolution in 1973 over President Nixon's veto as an attempt to reign in perceived transgressions of Executive powers. The Resolution states in pertinent part:

SECTION 1. This joint resolution may be cited as the "War Powers Resolution".

PURPOSE AND POLICY

SEC. 2. (a) It is the purpose of this joint resolution to fulfill the intent of the framers of the Constitution of the United States and insure that the collective judgment of both the Congress and the President will apply to the introduction of United States Armed Forces into hostilities, or into situations where imminent involvement in hostilities is clearly indicate by the circumstances, and to the continued use of such forces in hostilities or in such situations.

50 U.S.C. § 1543. REPORTING SEC. 4. (a) In the absence of a declaration of war, in any case in which United States Armed Forces are introduced — (1) into hostilities or into situations where imminent involvement in hostilities is clearly indicated by the circumstances; (2) into the territory, airspace or waters of a foreign nation, while equipped for combat, except for deployments which relate solely to supply, replacement, repair, or training of such forces; or (3) in numbers which substantially enlarge United States Armed Forces equipped for combat already located in a foreign nation; the president shall submit within 48 hours to the Speaker of the House of Representatives and to the President pro tempore of the Senate a report, in writing, setting forth — (A) the circumstances necessitating the introduction of United States Armed Forces; (B) the constitutional and legislative authority under which such introduction took place; and (C) the estimated scope and duration of the hostilities or involvement.

(b) The President shall provide such other information as the Congress may request in the fulfillment of its constitutional responsibilities with respect to committing the Nation to war and to the use of United States Armed Forces abroad

(c) Whenever United States Armed Forces are introduced into hostilities or into any situation described in subsection (a) of this section, the President shall, so long as such armed forces continue to be engaged in such hostilities or situation, report to the Congress periodically on the status of such hostilities or situation as well as on the scope and duration of such hostilities or situation, but in no event shall he report to the Congress less often than once every six months.

50 U.S.C. § 1544. CONGRESSIONAL ACTION SEC. 5. (a) Each report submitted pursuant to section 4(a)(1) shall be transmitted to the Speaker of the House of Representatives and to the President pro tempore of the Senate on the same calendar day. Each report so transmitted shall be referred to the Committee on Foreign Affairs of the House of Representatives and to the Committee on Foreign Relations of the Senate for appropriate action. If, when the report is transmitted, the Congress has adjourned sine die or has adjourned for any period in excess of three calendar days, the Speaker of the House of Representatives and the President pro tempore of the Senate, if they deem it advisable (or if petitioned by at least 30 percent of the membership of their respective Houses) shall jointly request the President to convene Congress in order that it may consider the report and take appropriate action pursuant to this section.

(b) Within sixty calendar days after a report is submitted or is required to be submitted pursuant to section 4(a)(1), whichever is earlier, the President shall terminate any use of United States Armed Forces with respect to which such report was submitted (or required to be submitted), unless the Congress (1) has declared war or has enacted a specific authorization for such use of United States Armed Forces, (2) has extended by law such sixty-day period, or (3) is physically unable to meet as a result of an armed attack upon the United States. Such sixty-day period shall be extended for not more than an additional thirty days if the President determines and certifies to the Congress in writing that unavoidable military necessity respecting the safety of United States Armed Forces requires the continued use of such armed forces in the course of bringing about a prompt removal of such forces.

(c) Notwithstanding subsection (b), at any time that United States Armed Forces are engaged in hostilities outside the territory of the United States, its possessions and territories without a declaration of war or specific statutory authorization, such forces shall be removed by the President if the Congress so directs by concurrent resolution. War Powers Resolution, Pub. L. No. 93-148, 87 Stat. 555 (1973).

EXERCISE 5.2: THE WAR POWERS RESOLUTION REVISITED AND REVISED

SKILLS AND VALUES UTILIZED:

- Interpreting statutes

ESTIMATED TIME FOR COMPLETION: 1 hour

LEVEL OF DIFFICULTY (1 to 5):

ROLE IN EXERCISE: You are the White House counsel.

EXERCISE: In the spring of 2011, President Obama committed United States troops to the NATO military air operation in Libya. If the actions involving United States support rose to the level of "hostilities" against Libya, the President was required under the War Powers Resolution to limit American participation or get the permission of Congress to continue such a mission. Instead, the President chose to interpret United States participation in a way that did not rise to the level of "hostilities", adopting the view of some of his advisors. *See* C. Savage, *2 Top Lawyers Lose Argument On War Power*, N.Y. Times, June 18, 2011, at A1, col. 2.

Somalia, a country in civil war since 1991, has been a "hot-spot" of instability monitored by other countries for a long time. Mogadishu, the capital, has been the subject of numerous incursions since that time. Somali pirates have hijacked numerous ships and kidnapped their occupants in the waters off of their country. Some of the pirates have raided nearby African nations, illustrated by two raids on neighboring Kenyan resorts. The coastline along Somalia is considered by the International Maritime Bureau to be some of the most dangerous coastline in the world.

To stop the lawlessness, the President intends to provide monetary aid and troops. The President would like to organize a coalition of African nations to help stop the lawlessness. The troops would be used to train others to maintain order, to protect against kidnapping, to help those kidnapped, and to protect American travel on the seas off of Somalia. Drones and air assistance would be provided as well. Any military personnel would be instructed that they were there to act as peacekeepers, and to fire only as a defensive maneuver. An air strike would occur only to protect civilians on the ground, such as in Libya.

The President has consulted with his advisors about the constitutionality of such actions. Several of the advisors have argued that the aggregate use of the armed forces, as well as the air strikes in particular, would violate the War Powers Resolution because they constituted "hostilities," triggering the Resolution. Others argued that the United States' role did not rise to "hostilities" under the War Powers Resolution.

Another group argued that the War Powers Resolution did not have a constitutional basis because it did not and could not spell out the dynamic boundary between the Congress and the Executive for protecting the United States.

Task: As the White House counsel, the President seeks your opinion about the scope of permissible constitutional action in light of the War Powers Resolution. While presidents have generally ignored the War Powers Resolution since its enactment, this President would like to propose a construction of the word "hostilities" that would clarify the line drawn by Congress and strengthen the legislative-executive interdependence dictated by the Constitution. This construction would be similar to a signing statement, which is a written comment on a law by a President at the time a law is signed. The comment often describes the President's interpretation of how the law should be interpreted and enforced. These signing statements have become very popular in the past several presidencies, but date back to Presidents James Monroe, Andrew Jackson and Ulysses S. Grant. The President would like the definition to exclude terrorism situations — but not action promoting stability in a region of the world on the premise that a single unstable country can threaten regional peace. The President would like your response by yesterday. (Okay, in an hour will suffice.)

Resources: Additional resources are available on the **LexisNexis Web Course** created for this book.

Chapter 6

THE "DORMANT" COMMERCE CLAUSE

INTRODUCTION

This chapter focuses on the dormant Commerce Clause, also commonly called the negative implications of the Commerce Clause. The judicially implied doctrine derives from the Commerce Clause, Article I, Section 8, Clause 3 of the Constitution. The name "dormant" comes from the fact that this doctrine applies to limit states when Congress is silent about the particular commercial activity in question.

The Supreme Court has held that the Commerce Clause does not give Congress exclusive power over commerce. *Gibbons v. Ogden*, 22 U.S. (Wheat) 1 (1824). Instead, the states sometimes have concurrent power to regulate commerce, even if that commerce impacts interstate commerce.

The dormant Commerce Clause claims a prominent place in the mosaic of most basic constitutional law courses. In some courses, the early dormant Commerce Clause rules of the 19th and 20th Centuries are discussed and vetted at length. In other courses, just the modern version of the doctrine is covered.

The "dormant" Commerce Clause often is paired with Congress' power under the Commerce Clause. Students sometimes blur the analysis of these very different mechanisms. Consequently, the first step in understanding this subject is to understand that the dormant Commerce Clause limits the powers of states, while the Commerce Clause is a source of power for Congress.

The regulation of commerce is not an intuitive subject for many students. After all, few people confront "dormant" clauses of any kind on a daily basis. The lack of intuitive parallels in real life makes the doctrine seem esoteric and elusive. The Supreme Court's use of balancing tests sometimes adds to the confusion. Yet, the dormant Commerce Clause connects to everyday life in several ways. For those students interested in history, the centuries-old doctrine has had an episodic and interesting past, not only for its varied iterations but also because it has mirrored the socio-economic, political and psychological history of various eras, such as the rise of the railroads in the late 1800s. Its long and winding judicial road is inextricably intertwined with the economic development of this country from an agrarian, to an industrial, to a post-industrial nation. Also, the doctrine provides a unique perspective of the legal difficulties that can arise from living in a crowded space with "neighbors," in this case sovereign states coexisting with other sovereign states. The doctrine reflects how difficult a task it is for courts to fashion workable limits on economic competition, while at the same time promoting a free marketplace.

While surprising to some, the doctrine is the subject of many legal disputes in the real world, perhaps more than most other constitutional law areas. The doctrine mediates conflicts between states and municipalities trying to grab commercial advantages in a competitive world. Like neighbors and siblings, sometimes the different sovereign entities don't play fairly with each other and the resulting dispute ends up in the courts.

As noted above, the federal-state power-sharing arrangement was advanced in the seminal case of *Gibbons v. Ogden*, 22 U.S. (9 Wheat) 1 (1824). In *Gibbons*, a New York statute provided Robert Livingston and Robert Fulton with the exclusive right to use steamboat transportation on several New York waterways. This exclusivity was challenged when Thomas Gibbons sought to use the same waterways for his own steamboats, based on a license granted by Congress. Justice John Marshall, using a fresh canvas once again, held that in the face of a conflict between federal and state authorization, the federal law reigns supreme. While the Court carved out an area of state control over completely internal matters, see, e.g., *Plumley v. Commonwealth of Massachusetts*, 155 U.S. 461 (1894), that included inspection and quarantine laws, see e.g., *Mintz v. Baldwin*, 289 U.S. 346 (1933), the Court left open the question of whether the states could share some of the power to regulate commerce to a later case, *Cooley v. Board of Wardens*, 53 U.S. 299 (1851). There, the Court found states could exercise concurrent commerce clause power alongside the federal government in matters of local regulation, so long as there were no conflicts. However, this power-sharing conception imposes significant limits on states, which are reflected in the dormant Commerce Clause doctrine.

The purposes of the limits on state regulation have been repeatedly stated. The limits are designed to promote economic equality among states in what and how they can regulate and to ensure that state regulations do not impede the free flow of the national economic system, especially by discriminating against or unduly burdening interstate commerce.

The doctrinal scheme has several layers. It starts with a question of federalism to determine whether the state regulation conflicts with or is preempted by a federal regulation. If there is a conflict or preemption by Congress, the state law generally will be struck down as unconstitutional. If there is no federal conflict or preemption, the analysis continues to the two major limits on state activity: whether the state laws discriminate against interstate commerce; or whether the laws unduly burden interstate commerce. The doctrinal structure is covered in greater detail below.

A. FEDERALISM — CONFLICT AND PREEMPTION

The predicate to the limits of dormant Commerce Clause analysis involves federalism, the relationship between federal and state governments. The federalism doctrine applies to dictate presumptive outcomes when federal and state governments have actual or potential conflicts. These actual or potential conflicts occur generally in three situations: "(1) where Congress has expressly preempted state law, (2) where Congress has legislated so comprehensively that federal law occupies an entire field of regulation and leaves no room for state law, or (3) where federal law conflicts with state law." *Wachovia Bank, N.A. v. Burke*, 414 F.3d 305, 313 (2d Cir. 2005). The key to

(2) above, or implied preemption, is the intent of Congress.

As noted above, if there is an express conflict between valid federal and state law, the federal law must prevail in a system governed by the Supremacy Clause of Article VI, Section 2. If there is no express conflict, the court will then address whether Congress expressly or impliedly intended through its own legislation to preempt the entire field of regulation, leaving no room for the states to legislate. The implied preemption concept is similar to a "no trespassing" sign placed on an owner's property, even if the owner is not using the property.

B.   LIMITS UNDER THE DORMANT COMMERCE CLAUSE

When Congress is silent, states are permitted to enact wide-ranging laws governing business, other economic matters or the movement of people. Yet, issues often arise between the state enacting a regulation and other impacted states concerning the same marketplace. These neighborly disputes are sometimes inevitable, given the other states' close proximity or the ready transportation of goods by plane, train, and truck between states, even those separated by thousands of miles.

Consequently, most of the dormant Commerce Clause litigation arises over state regulations that negatively impact the commerce of other states. The Supreme Court has declared that even when Congress is silent, there are limits on how a state can regulate commerce, even if that commerce physically occurs entirely within its own borders.

C.   LIMIT #1 ON STATE POWER OVER REGULATION OF LOCAL COMMERCE: NO DISCRIMINATION

This limit prohibits states from discriminating against interstate commerce to promote a market economy and protect against home-state favoritism, either in its means or ends. States cannot favor their own commerce in design or impact, despite laws qualifying as health, welfare or safety measures otherwise within the states' police powers. States cannot likewise disfavor the economic functioning of other states. For example, in *Healy v. Beer Institute*, 491 U.S. 324 (1989), a state law was found by the Supreme Court to be unconstitutional because the law attempted to control commercial activity occurring entirely outside of the regulating state.

Overt discrimination is often justified by states based on neutral grounds. A leading case in this area is *City of Philadelphia v. New Jersey*, 437 U.S. 617 (1978). In City of Philadelphia, a New Jersey law prohibiting the importation of various kinds of waste was challenged by private landfill owners in New Jersey as well as the City of Philadelphia. Although the law was justified based on environmental concerns, the Supreme Court held that such overt discrimination was impermissible. The Commerce Clause protected Philadelphia "from efforts by one State to isolate itself in the stream of interstate commerce from a problem shared by all." *Id.* at 627.

Facial neutrality predominates in most state laws, since states do not want to cast themselves as parochial by enacting laws evidencing blatant favoritism of their own commerce over that of other states. Over the years, another branch of the analysis arose, involving discrimination in a law's results.

Regardless of whether the discrimination occurred in design or outcome, the court will strike the law down unless the state meets a form of heightened scrutiny through an important state interest and a showing of no less discriminatory alternatives. *Dean Milk Co. v. City of Madison*, 340 U.S. 349 (1951). In *Dean Milk*, the City of Madison, Wisconsin enacted an ordinance that required pasteurization of milk to be sold in the city at an approved plant located within five miles of the city center. The Court considered and struck down the five-mile limit, finding that it circumvented competition by "erecting an economic barrier." *Id.* The Court then concluded that "reasonable and adequate alternatives are available" to the provision and could have been enacted.

D.   LIMIT #2: NO UNDUE BURDEN ON INTERSTATE COMMERCE

This second major limit prohibits states from acting in a way that unduly burdens interstate commerce. The Court utilizes a balancing test derived from *Pike v. Bruce Church, Inc.*, 397 U.S. 137 (1970) to determine whether a burden created by a law is undue. The *Pike* balancing test only applies when the state law is nondiscriminatory. This means that the law does not engage in differential treatment of in-state and out-of-state commercial interests. *Pike* stated that a nondiscriminatory law would be upheld "unless the burden imposed on such commerce is clearly excessive in relation to the putative local benefits." *Pike*, 397 U.S. at 142. Thus, *Pike* required the courts to balance the impact of the law on interstate commerce against the benefits to the regulating state. If the law unduly burdens interstate commerce, it is struck down, regardless of its evenhandedness between states.

E.   EXCEPTIONS TO LIMITS

There are several important exceptions to the limits generally imposed by the Commerce Clause. One exception concerns the prohibition against state discrimination of interstate commerce. States still can regulate commerce in a discriminatory manner if invited to do so by Congress, if the states demonstrate a substantial state interest for doing so and no lesser restrictive alternative, or if the state is acting as a market participant. A market participant acts by buying and selling in the marketplace instead of supervising the market as a regulator. In *South-Central Timber Development, Inc., v. Wunnicke*, 467 U.S. 82 (1984), for example, Alaska sold its own timber to residents at a favorable rate. The Supreme Court held that when a state enters the market as a seller of its own goods and services, it can properly favor its own residents. Significantly, though, the Court found that Alaska went too far by imposing additional "downstream" restrictions on the timber once Alaska had sold it. Those "downstream" restrictions that occurred post-sale were found to be unconstitutional.

EXERCISE 6.1: RED, RED WINE

SKILLS AND VALUES UTILIZED:

- Decision-making and judgment
- Efficiency and relevancy in a client interview
- Ethics — conflict of interest

ESTIMATED TIME FOR COMPLETION: 1 hour.

LEVEL OF DIFFICULTY (1 to 5):

ROLE IN EXERCISE: You are an attorney for the Plaintiff wishing to challenge the state law's constitutionality under the dormant Commerce Clause.

TASK: Conducting a client interview, and choosing relevant and important questions to ask.

BACKGROUND INFORMATION: The State of North Carolina has its own mini "wine country" — a series of small farm vineyards in the northern and western parts of the state. These vineyards sell to retailers and wholesalers around the state, the country and the world. One vineyard is the Yistoya Vineyards. This family-owned small farm vineyard has operated as such for 90 years. Yistoya sells a variety of wines, mostly cabernets, merlots, and wine blends.

The State of North Carolina limits the sale of alcoholic beverages based on the 21st Amendment to the United States Constitution and its own police powers of health, safety, welfare and morals. The limits are contained in the State's Alcoholic Beverage Control Act, which establishes a three-tier system for the distribution of alcohol within the state. Tier One of the system focuses on the manufacturers of wine and other alcohol. Tier Two concerns the wholesalers of wine and other alcohol and Tier Three involves the retailers.

The law permits manufacturers of wine to sell and ship wines only to licensed in-state wholesalers. These licensed wholesalers, in turn, may sell only to licensed in-state retailers. Shippers must obtain a shipping license in accordance with the law. Any other kinds of shipments, whether direct from manufacturer to retailer or manufacturer to consumer, are prohibited, with limited exceptions.

The law applies to wineries located in the State of North Carolina and out-of-state. While the law appeared to function well, local wineries like the Yistoya vineyards were unhappy with it. In the spring and summer, Yistoya had many visitors who wished to sample and purchase its wine. Under the law as written, the vineyards were prohibited from being a point of purchase, i.e., no retail sale of wine could take place at a vineyard.

The manager of Yistoya, Ned Smirnov, was quoted in an interview with the local newspaper as saying, "Visitors spend good money and effort to visit us and are then told they now have to leave and find a retailer to purchase wine they can see being prepared by us. It takes away from the whole experience here. It makes no sense."

After other such interviews with vineyard owners, complaints by wine enthusiasts and lobbying efforts in the state legislature, the legislature enacted the North Carolina Small Farm Wine Law. According to the Director of the North Carolina Alcoholic Beverage Control Division, Albert Moore, this amendment to the existing law permitted small in-state wineries (such as Yistoya) to sell and ship wine directly to consumers and retailers in the state, bypassing wholesalers completely. Small wineries were defined in the law as those that sold fewer than 250,000 gallons of wine a year.

The NC Code Ann. Section 2-4-16002, stated in pertinent part: "Small farm wineries as defined below may sell their wines on premises for consumption on or off premises between the hours of 11 a.m. and 5 p.m. EST year-round."

Yistoya Vineyards began having fee-based wine tasting events, as well as in-person sales of bottles and cases of wine directly to visiting consumers. The in-person sales were very successful and became a strong base of revenue for the local vineyards.

Arnold Passat, a resident of Raleigh, NC, visited the Yistoya Vineyards and bought several cases of wine on the premises. Arnold purchased the cases after buying several glasses of Merlot wine for the sum of $9.99. Another visitor, Susan Masterson, purchased two cases of merlot, which she promptly took directly to her home in Harrisburg, Pennsylvania. Sharon Anderson visited Yistoya the same day and purchased a sample flute of five wines for $15.99. Sharon and four friends consumed the wine in the Yistoya wine-tasting room while watching television and eating free cheese dip and crackers. Anyone else of the legal drinking age visiting the farm could purchase the wine on the premises for drinking on-site.

Arnold Passat was no casual wine drinker, but a hardcore fan of local wineries. He wished to order wine from a similar small farm winery, the Wolverine Winery, located in Michigan's Upper Peninsula. The North Carolina law prevented Arnold from doing so, despite Wolverine's willingness to ship wine to him directly. Arnold is unhappy, because he must travel to Michigan to purchase the wine or buy it from a licensed retailer in the State of North Carolina at a marked-up retail price.

You had become familiar with the North Carolina law several months ago. You recognize the advantages created by the law's small farm exception, but also understand that the market for on-site purchase may be different than the market for purchases in wine stores containing all kinds and labels of wines. The travel issue bugs you a little, though — does it advantage or merely distinguish the purchases of small farm wines?

You also note that while the 21st Amendment creates the basis for much of the legal analysis associated with alcoholic beverage-related state legislation, it does not impact the analysis here, which is based on the dormant Commerce Clause. Thus, you are instructed to properly ignore the 21st Amendment in this problem.

Arnold has come to you for representation. Your law clerk has prepared a list of questions to ask Arnold in your first meeting with him. You know that a client interview serves three purposes — to get information, to give information and to develop rapport. It is important to obtain the factual parameters of the case to determine whether the case has merit and to begin developing strategies and tactics. It is important to provide the client with information about the process so his or her expectations are not unrealistic. Finally, the attorney-client relationship can be an attribute or hindrance in a case and it is important for the attorney to maximize channels for communication with a client.

EXERCISE: Your job is to select the top five questions to ask from those provided below, and to explain why those questions are important in the context of this case. The list of questions provided by the law clerk follows.

1. Arnold, what happened that caused you to want to bring this lawsuit?

2. How often do you drink wine?

3. What do you see as the important issues in this case?

4. What is your favorite wine?

5. Have you ever been involved in a lawsuit before? If yes, please explain your involvement.

6. Why do you visit wineries?

7. Would you like to hear about the main issues in the case?

8. Have you ever been convicted of any crimes?

9. Would you mind if I represent the Wolverine Winery in Michigan as well as you?

10. How are you going to pay for my legal services?

11. Would you like to know what you can expect if I represent you?

EXERCISE 6.2: THE MINNESOTA GIFT CARD LAW

This problem asks students to focus on the nuances of the dormant Commerce Clause. This implied doctrine, also called the negative implications of the Commerce Clause, serves as a limit on state regulation of commerce. In essence, the provision acts as a traffic officer, making sure American commerce highways and by-ways are free flowing.

SKILLS AND VALUES UTILIZED:

- Formulating deposition questions.

- Communicating doctrinal understanding in bullet points

- Negotiation

ESTIMATED TIME FOR COMPLETION: 1 hour.

LEVEL OF DIFFICULTY (1 to 5):

ROLE IN EXERCISE: You are an Assistant Attorney General, one of the lead counsel for the State of Minnesota.

TASK: Providing advocacy advice for the State.

BACKGROUND INFORMATION: The Attorney General is being sued to prevent the enforcement of the Minnesota gift card law, detailed below. You are to provide advice about how to defend the suit in *Minnesota Maximus Mall v. Attorney General of Minnesota.*

1. The Minnesota Maximus Mall Gift Card

The Card. Plastic, bright blue. Includes dollar amounts in each corner. States the applicable rules in small print on the back. Says in larger print, "Good at all Mall locations. Special discounts also available at select locations."

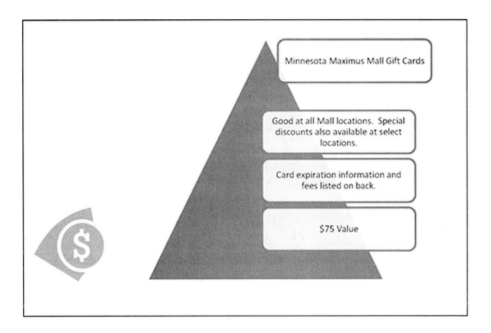

2. Gift Card Rules

The following statement appears on the back of the cards:

The Maximus Mall Gift Cards can be purchased at any designated store or facility in the Maximus Mall. The cards expire one-year from the date of issue. There is a monthly inactivity "service" charge of $1.50 per card for each calendar month the card is not in use. The fee will be automatically assessed. The cards are supported by the BDA Bank, a national banking institution, and operate like a debit card, using the same kind of platform. BDA bank has reviewed and approved the terms of the cards, and has been paid for setting up the card and providing the debit card services. BDA, however, while technically issuing the cards, are really only providing some services in support of the cards. The gift cards instead, are offered to consumers exclusively by the Minnesota Maximus Mall, a private limited liability company, and not by the bank. There shall be a $5.00 charge to reissue lost cards. If the card expires, the balance on the card can be transferred to a completely new card, subject to a $7.50 reissuance fee.

3. Pertinent Law

Minnesota State Law 4-11-C: "No gift cards or certificates offered in the State shall be subject to inactivity or dormancy fees or an expiration date."

Federal Law: The National Banking Act, 12 U.S.C. Section 24 et seq., permits national banks to operate with several explicit powers regarding the issuance of credit or debit cards and implied powers "necessary to carry on the business of banking," including the offering of "electronic stored value systems." 12 C.F.R. Section 7.5002(a)(3). These value systems, including the debit card network utilized by the Minnesota Mall for its cards, allow consumers to accumulate pre-paid value in cards outside of a conventional bank account and do not have stated limits on whether banks can include expiration dates or inactivity fees.

4. Additional Background Information

Gift cards are big business. Consumers in the calendar year 2006 purchased approximately $80 billion worth of gift cards. Of that, around $8 billion will never be redeemed. *See, e.g.*, Mark Chediak, *Darden to Repay Fees on Gift Cards for Its Restaurants*, ORLANDO SENTINEL, Apr. 4, 2007 at A1. To protect consumers, several states enacted laws limiting expiration and inactivity fees.

Unfortunately for consumers, the nature of the card issuer can make a difference in whether expiration dates and inactivity fees are valid. As one commentator noted:

> Even though retailers may stop imposing service fees and expiration dates in compliance with state law, many retailers may also choose to avoid state laws by letting national banks issue their gift cards and taking a commission from the banks. [T]he National Bank Act, [12 U.S.C. Section 21 et seq.], which governs nationally chartered banks, allows banks to charge fees of their choosing for their banking products, including gift cards. The National Bank Act was designed to create uniformity of national bank regulation and preempts any state law attempting to regulate national banks that conflicts with the main objectives of the Act.

Y. Angela Lam, Note, *The Gift That Keeps on Taking: How Federal Banking Laws Prevent States from Enforcing Gift Card Laws*, 93 MINN. L. REV. 311, 313 (2007).

There is at least one court that supports the thesis that the National Bank Act preempts state regulation regarding both expiration dates and fees, *LLC v. Ayotte*, 488 F.3d 525, 531-532 (1st Cir. 2007), *cert. denied*, 128 S. Ct. 1258 (2008) but another court concluded that the National Bank Act limits expiration date legislation by states, but does not limit service fee regulation. *SPGGC, LLC v. Blumenthal*, 505 F.3d 183, 191–92 (2d Cir. 2007).

Maximus Mall owner, Dan Weston, noted in an interview: "We have used this mall value card with inactivity service fees and expiration dates in Minnesota and other states with great success for several years. Just last year we issued such a card at our Ohio Maximus Mall. These cards are especially useful during the holidays and for business at other times generally. If this law is strictly construed it would not only hurt us, but lots of commerce within this state would be chilled. To that end, the Minnesota law negatively impacts interstate commerce because it conflicts with the regulations of other states.

The Attorney General offered a written statement: "We interpret the State of Minnesota law to prohibit the sale of gift cards by retailers within the state when those cards have inactivity fees or expiration dates. It is noteworthy that the Minnesota law does not apply to cards that are purchased out-of-state and used in Minnesota. Thus, it is important to emphasize the law deals only with sales and not use. The object of the law is to protect Minnesota consumers from unknowingly draining the value of cards purchased in the state. Sometimes that fine print is so fine it is hard to understand."

EXERCISE: The Attorney General (AG) approaches you, an Assistant Attorney General for the State of Minnesota, with three requests:

(1)   The AG asks you to meet with the first assistant AG, who is involved in negotiations on this case with the Mall, to provide a list of "talking points" on preemption and why it should not apply here. The Attorney General concedes that there might indeed be preemption of the Minnesota law if the BNA bank had issued the gift cards directly or was a true national bank. The AG distinguishes that kind of case from this one based on the fact that the Mall is a retail facility and the BNA bank is only providing support to a private company. The AG asks you whether you thought this distinction is valid and explain this issue to the first assistant AG.

(2)   The AG also asks whether you could you be responsible for part of the deposition of Dan Weston, the Maximus Mall owner. The AG wants you to write 15 questions, half advocacy questions (meaning they are leading, suggesting a yes or no answer), and half inquiry questions (meaning they are open-ended and do not suggest an answer) about the question of the law's discrimination. The AG wants you to obtain useful facts about the preemption issue and the question of whether the law discriminates against interstate commerce. You can ask 5 advocacy questions about preemption and five inquiry questions about discrimination. These questions should either pin the owner down or offer useful additional information. After you choose the questions, explain why you are asking these questions.

(3)   If both sides would be better off settling the case, what would you offer if you were given the authority to do so? What are some of the strengths and weaknesses of the case you would consider in determining what offer you would make to settle the case?

EXERCISE 6.3: FOG LIGHTS

SKILLS AND VALUES UTILIZED:

- Persuasive advocacy
- Organization and relevancy of questioning

ESTIMATED TIME FOR COMPLETION: 1 hour.

LEVEL OF DIFFICULTY (1 to 5):

ROLE IN EXERCISE: You are an attorney in the law firm of Dexter, Chatham, which represents the plaintiff, Billy Bobbly Trucking (BBT) Company, a nation-wide trucking concern, in a recently filed lawsuit against the State of Kentucky Transportation Department.

TASK: Creating effective deposition questions.

BACKGROUND INFORMATION: The State of Kentucky enacts a law, 12-D-6(a), that states in part: "All trucks using state highways and byways must be equipped with a minimum of the following devices to promote safety on the roads:

i.   Four (4) reflectors placed on the four corners of the truck in the rear;

ii.   Three (3) blinking reflectors in the rear indicating braking action;

iii. Six (6) other reflector devices, three (3) per side, that will have automatic battery or electric operation upon nightfall; and

iv.   Special sustainable ultra-beam quality front fog lights for the front that will be operable in all foggy conditions."

The cost of the safety devices per truck is approximately $1195, with the high-technology fog lights accounting for most of the expense. The other devices require special wiring, which adds labor costs to their instillation. Several trucking companies have these or equivalent devices, but the majority do not. One other state, Indiana, is considering implementing a similar law, but has not yet done so.

BBT runs trucks regularly through Kentucky on their coast-to-coast runs. To navigate around the State would add an extra 200 minutes to the route, which occurs at least twice a day. There would be an extra $80 in gasoline for the extra time used, and $100 per driver. The extra wear on the tires would be an issue and drivers would become increasingly tired at the end of the long haul. To rig all 89 trucks in the BBT fleet with the special safety devices would be very costly to BBT, an extra expense it does not want to make.

BBT sues the Kentucky Transportation Department in Federal District Court claiming Kentucky's alleged safety law violates the dormant Commerce Clause. The case is set for trial and pre-trial discovery commences.

EXERCISE: The State Attorney General intends to offer an expert witness on transportation safety, Dr. Sam Safi. In a deposition, Dr. Safi says trucks are definitely at a lower risk of an accident with the protective devices than without them. How much of a lower risk, the witness could not precisely say. Dr. Safi did say that in foggy conditions, such marking have been shown to reduce accidents by 18 percent, with a total of 10 fewer accidents per year involving commercial trucks statewide.

Partially in rebuttal, the plaintiff BBT intends to offer a meteorologist, Dr. Marty Metrist, who has a Ph.D. in meteorology with a B.A. majoring in physics and mathematics. Metrist will testify that the use of fog lights is helpful to truckers on average fewer than 6 times a year per trucker on the state highways, as well as other important information. [See the chart below.] Based on the data in the chart and his experience and training, Dr. Metrist concludes that the law creates only a "marginally safer" road system.

fog light use on state highways: 6 per year average	fog light use on other state roads: 8.3 per year average	fog light use in hilly state terrain: 12 per year average
fog light use on flat terrain: 5 per year average	fog light use by season: varies by 25 percent	

Question #1: How would you write out Dr. Metrist's testimony if you were assigned to do the direct examination of him? Note that a direct examination of an expert is designed to do the following: 1. Introduce the witness, through his background and credentials to build credibility and qualify him or her as an expert; 2. Show the factual basis of the witness's conclusions; and 3. Provide a conclusion that adds to your case or diminishes the opposition's case. This three-part structure helps to build an expert witness's effect on a jury. In a sense, the expert offers a reality normally not possessed by jurors. On direct examination, non-leading questions are the norm. A non-leading question does not suggest an answer and is typified by questions beginning with "What?" "When?" "How?" "Where?" and "Why?" For example, asking Dr. Metrist, "Why did you reach that conclusion?" is a non-leading question. Write out a brief direct examination.

Question #2: How would the State likely cross-examine Dr. Metrist? Write out a brief set of cross-examination questions. On cross-examination, it is worth noting that questions can be and usually are leading, meaning the questions suggest an answer.

Leading questions often call for a "yes" or "no" response. For example, "You went to the store, right?" is a leading question, suggesting that the respondent went to the store.

Question #3: How would you use Dr. Metrist's testimony in your closing argument in the case? The closing argument attempts to show that the evidentiary burden has been met by your client (if it had the burden), in part because the testimony presented is credible and useful. Thus, how would Dr. Metrist's testimony be most helpful to BBT?

Chapter 7

PROCEDURAL DUE PROCESS

INTRODUCTION

There are two due process clauses in the Constitution: the clause in the Fifth Amendment applies to the federal government and the clause in the Fourteenth Amendment applies to state and local governments. Each clause has two constitutional dimensions: substantive due process and procedural due process. (Only lawyers could distinguish between the first dimension — "substantive process" is something of a contradiction — and the second dimension — "process process" is something of a redundancy. But so be it.) If the government — federal, state, or local — affords a person "due process of law" then the government may constitutionally deprive the person of "life, liberty, or property." Thus, the government's sovereign power hangs over all our heads, like the sword of Damocles, suspended merely by a hair of process.

Therefore, Justice Marshall was not exaggerating to exclaim that "it is procedural due process that is our fundamental guarantee of fairness, our protection against arbitrary, capricious, and unreasonable governmental action . . . ." *Board of Regents v. Roth*, 408 U.S. 564, 589 (1972) (Marshall, J., dissenting). The remedy for a denial of procedural due process is to be afforded adequate and sufficient process, i.e., adequate notice and a meaningful opportunity to be heard. The modern procedural due process analysis asks and answers two straightforward questions in sequence. The first question is: did the government deprive a person of something that is "life" or "liberty" or "property"? If the answer is "yes," then the second question is: what process is due and when?

Understand that "life, liberty, and property" are not guaranteed; only "process" is guaranteed. Thus, the due process clauses ultimately are draconian provisions. Consider the ultimate power over life and death. If the state affords a person the full panoply of procedural due process, the state can deprive a person of life itself. *See Gregg v. Georgia*, 428 U.S. 153 (1976) (upholding the constitutionality of the death penalty). According to the Supreme Court, the Constitution does not answer the philosophical and religious question of when life begins, *Roe v. Wade*, 410 U.S. 113, 159 (1973), and has little to say about how life should end, see *Vacco v. Quill*, 521 U.S. 793, 807-08 (1997). "Liberty" or "property" is what is at stake in most procedural due process cases. "Liberty" has its origin in the Constitution, in the substantive rights protected by the Bill of Rights and the Fourteenth Amendment. Liberty thus defies simple definition. It includes those rights and privileges recognized to be essential to the orderly pursuit of happiness. "Property" is not created by the Constitution; property is more than a personal abstract need or desire; property is a legitimate claim of entitlement of the kind that people reasonably rely on in their everyday lives; property has its origin in some independent source such as state law, for example, the law of contracts or the law of property or statutes and regulations establishing governmental entitlements and licenses. *See Board of Regents v. Roth*, 408 U.S. 564 (1972); *Perry v. Sindermann*, 408 U.S. 593 (1972).

Again, procedural due process is a guarantee of process, not a guarantee of any particular outcome or result, i.e., if you prevail with a procedural due process argument, your remedy is adequate and effective notice plus a fair and reasonable opportunity to be heard in a meaningful manner. You may still lose on the merits of your claim. The timing of the hearing — whether the hearing must take place before the deprivation or after the deprivation or in some combination of before and after — is a related, much litigated question. The Supreme Court drew a guideline in two leading cases.

In *Goldberg v. Kelly*, 397 U.S. 254 (1970), the Supreme Court applied a balancing analysis to decide that a state had to hold a pre-termination proceeding and provide a more formal, quasi-judicial evidentiary hearing before cutting off public assistance payments to a welfare recipient. The majority emphasized the "brutal need" of basic subsistence on the side of the individual over the interest of conserving fiscal and administrative resources on the government's side of the balance.

That holding was distinguished but not overruled in *Mathews v. Eldridge*, 424 U.S. 319 (1976), which upheld a less formal proceeding before terminating Social Security disability payments. The majority deemed the individual interest to be somewhat greater in the welfare benefits case. The majority also reasoned that the evidence and the nature of the issues to be determined in the two cases were constitutionally different; the issue of determining eligibility for welfare was open-ended and highly-contestable but the issue of determining medical disability was factual, scientific and subject to medical tests and professional expertise. Consequently, in *Mathews*, the majority revised the balancing analysis into a three-factor analysis to determine what process is due: (1) the private individual interest being affected; (2) the risk of error in the procedures that were followed versus the probable value of additional or substitute procedures; and (3) the government's interest. That is the formal analysis.

The first factor is almost always on the individual's side marshaling in favor of earlier and more procedures. The third factor is mostly on the government's side marshaling in favor of later and lesser procedures. [However, at times the Court is willing to find a government interest favoring *more* process. *See, e.g., Cleveland Bd. of Educ. v. Loudermill*, 470 U.S. 532 (1985) (recognizing that the government employer had an interest in avoiding unnecessary disruption and erroneous dismissals).] It is the second factor that can move the balance of interests in either direction: in favor of the individual and more process or in favor of the government and less process. The Supreme Court candidly has admitted that this three-factor analysis is not an "all embracing test for deciding due process claims," but rather the due process clause ultimately requires a "straightforward test of reasonableness under the circumstances." *Dusenbery v. United States*, 534 U.S. 161, 167-68 (2002). The law has come full circle now that the justices have called on the lower courts to assess the ultimate fairness of the actual process which has been afforded by the government compared to the promise of greater fairness from adding the additional process that the individual is requesting. The requirements of procedural due process are determined on a case-by-case, interest-by-interest basis by examining what is at stake for the individual and the government.

EXERCISE 7.1: DRAFTING A LAW SCHOOL GRADE APPEAL POLICY

SKILLS AND VALUES UTILIZED:

- Case analysis and synthesis

- Gathering and sorting exemplars of grade appeal policies to arrive at a sense of the "best practices" in legal education

- Understanding and appreciating the practicalities of constitutional doctrine

- Institution building and systems design

- Developing a consensus policy that is straightforward, efficient, reasonable, and fair to students and faculty

ESTIMATED TIME FOR COMPLETION: Approximately 1 1/2 hours.

LEVEL OF DIFFICULTY (1 to 5):

TASK: Suppose you are a member of the founding faculty of Portia School of Law at State University, a newly-established public law school. The dean appoints you to a committee to draft a grade appeal policy because you are a noted con law professor. You are in the philosophical middle of the three-professor committee. Your faculty colleague, Professor Ardtest, who is a very conservative traditionalist, is skeptical and cynical about grade appeal policies because she believes that such policies have the pernicious potential to compromise a grading professor's academic freedom to evaluate students and assign grades. She favors writing a D+ grade appeal procedure, the minimum process that will pass a constitutional challenge under the Fourteenth Amendment. Your other faculty colleague, Professor Blednart, who is a very liberal critical legal theorist, regrets the illegitimate hierarchy of grades and grading because he believes that law school grades too often amount to acts of unconscious aggression which harm students and interfere with the deeper relationship of teacher and student. He is in favor of affording law students "undue process," more than the Fourteenth Amendment would require. Therefore, whatever procedures you propose will have at least one additional vote, so you can broker the kind of policy you yourself think is best for teachers and students. Your draft is certain to get out of committee for a faculty vote.

Open your preferred internet browser and perform a search with the search terms: "grade appeal + procedure + law school + student + faculty." Take 20 minutes to study and review some examples of existing grade appeal procedures at various law schools around the United States. Determine what features they have in common. Pick and choose those features that commend themselves to your innate sense of fairness and reasonableness. Draft a grade appeal policy for the Portia School of Law taking into account the *Mathews v. Eldridge* three-factor analysis outlined in the INTRO-DUCTION. Then take a moment to compare your draft to the actual grade appeal procedures at your own law school.

EXERCISE 7.2: CONTESTING A BENEFITS CUT-OFF

SKILLS AND VALUES UTILIZED:

- Explanation of Legal Concepts
- Fact Development

GENERAL DESCRIPTION OF EXERCISE: Explaining the law to a layperson client, and interviewing the client to develop legally-relevant facts.

PARTICIPANTS NEEDED: This exercise is best performed in groups of 2-4.

ESTIMATED TIME FOR COMPLETION: 1 hour

LEVEL OF DIFFICULTY (1 to 5):

ROLE IN EXERCISE: Attorney for client.

Note: The following fact pattern involves the federal Medicare program. You should assume that the statement of the program provided in the question is accurate — in other words, don't import any knowledge you may have of the actual program if it conflicts with this question's statement of how the program works.

BACKGROUND INFORMATION: The federal government, through its Medicare program, reimburses certain medical expenses incurred by senior citizens. Over the past decade, a new treatment has arisen for back pain, called "whole body therapy," or "WBT." WBT involves a combination of drug therapy, massage and so-called "relaxation classes," where people are taught breathing and mind-control techniques (i.e., techniques that are claimed allow a person to control one's perceptions of pain). WBT has been pioneered by storefront "pain clinics" that have sprung up in areas of high senior citizen population, especially Florida and Arizona.

Last week, WBT Services of Miami Beach ("WBT Services"), a WBT clinic in Miami Beach, received the letter, reprinted as Appendix A, from the federal agency responsible for administering the Medicare program. As you'll see, the letter informs WBT Services that it is being terminated as an "Approved Medicare Provider." "Approved Medicare Provider" status is necessary before the Medicare Program will reimburse the provider for services provided to Medicare patients. The letter accuses WBT Services of providing unnecessary treatment — in particular, treatment to people who have already recovered from their pain conditions. Bill Berman, the President of WBT Services, believes that treatment after self-reported recovery is appropriate, because many pain patients report cures, supported by standard medical diagnostic information, only to suffer relapses unless several additional rounds of therapy are provided. As Berman explained when he first called your law office, the entire basis of WBT is the theory that patients must acknowledge that their pain exists — and then to acknowledge that it has left. Indeed, a standard part of the therapy is a "pain farewell session," conducted six weeks after the last reported incidence of pain.

Berman is worried that the procedures set forth in the letter and the Medicare statute (Appendix B) will deprive him of Medicare income for so long that he will have to go out of business. He wishes to challenge those procedures as inadequate.

You have scheduled an appointment with Berman, one hour from now.

TASK 1: Draft a brief computer slide (e.g., Power Point) presentation for him that explains whether or not his continued eligibility to participate in the Medicare program as a provider is an interest protected by the constitutional guarantee of procedural due process.

TASK 2: Assume that the answer to the first question is "yes." Develop a series of questions for Berman that will help you determine more conclusively if the procedures in the statute and the letter are constitutional. Next to each question, place a brief notation explaining why the question is relevant, in case he asks.

APPENDIX A

Letter from the Agency to WBT Services of Miami Beach, Inc.

VIA CERTIFIED MAIL

Dear Dr. Berman:

This letter informs you that, as of your receipt of this letter, the Administrator of the Medicare Program has determined that you are in violation of the Medicare statute. In particular, the Administrator has determined that you have engaged in "inappropriate medical practices," as that term is set forth in Section 804(a) of the Medicare Act. Specifically, the Administrator believes that you have provided pain-treatment services, and sought Medicare reimbursement for those services, after patients have reported a complete cure of their previous pain conditions.

If you wish to contest this determination, please refer to Section 804 of the Medicare Act, which provides the procedures for appealing such determinations.

Finally, note that current backlogs in processing appeals from revocations of Provider status mean that First Stage Appeals (defined in the statute) generally take 2-3 months to process. Further, Second Stage Appeals (again, defined in the statute) generally take 6-12 months to schedule. You may not request scheduling of a Second Stage Appeal until your First Stage Appeal has been denied.

Sincerely,

J.T. Tremaine
Regional Director of Provider Services

APPENDIX B

Excerpts from the Federal Medicare Law

TITLE II: BASIC PROVISIONS . . .

Section 204: Covered Treatments

The Administrator of the Medicare Program ("Administrator") shall establish a list of medically appropriate treatments. Only medically appropriate treatments shall be reimbursed by Medicare . . . .

TITLE VIII: AUTHORIZED MEDICARE PROVIDERS . . .

Section 803: Providers

Only Authorized Medicare Providers shall be eligible to receive reimbursement for services provided to persons insured by Medicare. Such Authorized Medicare Providers shall be entitled to prompt reimbursement for expenses charged in the course of providing legally-reimbursable medical services.

Section 804: Termination of Approved Medicare Provider Status

(a) If the Administrator determines that an Authorized Medicare Provider ("Provider") has engaged in fraud or inappropriate medical practices, he shall terminate his status as a Provider.

(b) If the Administrator determines that such a termination is appropriate, he shall inform the Provider as soon as practicable by certified mail.

(c) A Provider notified of termination as set forth in subsection (b) may contest the termination in two steps:

(i) *First Stage Appeal:* If the Provider wishes to contest such a termination decision, it may first send documentation to the Administrator setting forth its argument and providing documentary support.

(ii) *Second Stage Appeal:* If the Administrator rejects the Provider's argument or disagrees with the documentary support in the First Stage Appeal, the Provider may request an oral hearing before an official of the Program. At that hearing the Provider may testify, and he may call any witnesses s/he wishes.

(d) The Provider shall remain eligible to perform services for Medicare reimbursement during the First Stage Appeal. If that appeal is rejected, the Provider shall be deemed ineligible for reimbursement of services performed after date of that rejection. If the Second Stage Appeal is successful, the agency shall notify the Provider that it is again an Authorized Medicare Provider. Only upon receipt of that notification shall the Provider be allowed to perform medical services for reimbursement by Medicare.

Chapter 8

IS THERE A RIGHT TO DIE?

INTRODUCTION

Is there a right to die protected in the Constitution? Certainly, the substantive due process guarantee in the 14th Amendment protects a person's freedom to refuse unwanted medical treatment. This freedom was also protected at common law. The Supreme Court has long recognized that a person has an individual liberty interest to reject unwanted medical care. *See Vitek, Correctional Director v. Jones*, 445 U.S. 480 (1980). But what does the right to refuse medical care really mean? Does it include a right to die? Should it? And if so, how far should this right extend? Though sometimes characterized as the liberty to be free from state interference, the Court now understands this interest to be an individual liberty interest in personal autonomy.

But what are the limits of the right to refuse medical treatment? Does a competent person have a right to refuse life-sustaining medical treatment? The Court assumed the existence of this right in *Cruzan v. Director, Missouri Department of Health*, 497 U.S. 261 (1990). *Cruzan* is focused primarily on the procedural safeguards needed to invoke the right to refuse medical treatment, including life-saving measures. The case involved Nancy Cruzan, a woman in a persistent vegetative state who could not express her wishes and did not make an advance determination before her car accident whether she wanted to be kept artificially alive. The Court held Missouri could stop Nancy Cruzan's parents from ordering the withholding of food and water from their daughter unless there was "clear and convincing" evidence that she would have wanted to die. *Cruzan* therefore suggests that there is a right to refuse life-sustaining measures such as hydration and nutrition and the Court has reinforced this constitutional assumption in two subsequent cases: *Washington v. Glucksberg*, 521 U.S. 702 (1997) and *Vacco v. Quill*, 521 U.S. 793 (1997).

Is there, then, a broad, general right to die, i.e., a right to determine how and when to end your life? Not necessarily. The right to commit suicide or the right to obtain the assistance of someone else to commit suicide is not "deeply rooted in this Nation's history and tradition" and therefore not regarded with the same constitutional respect and deference as the right to refuse medical treatment. State laws on assisted suicide are constitutional provided they are rationally related to a legitimate state interest. The Supreme Court has found that the state has several legitimate state interests that justify regulating or even prohibiting assisted suicide: "(1) preserving life; (2) preventing suicide; (3) avoiding the involvement of third parties and the use of arbitrary, unfair, or undue influence; (4) protecting family members or loved ones; (5) protecting the integrity of the medical profession; and (6) avoiding future movement toward euthanasia and other abuses." *Washington v. Glucksberg*, 521 U.S. 702 (1997), at 728 note 20.

EXERCISE 8.1: DIFFICULT DECISIONS

SUBSTANTIVE CONTENT:

- Introduction to right to refuse (life-saving) medical treatment
- Discussion of standards of proof

SKILLS AND VALUES UTILIZED:

- Doctrinal knowledge
- Oral advocacy
- Statutory drafting
- Problem-solving
- Negotiation and Collaboration

GENERAL DESCRIPTION OF EXERCISE:

TASK 1: "The Great Debate."

Your team will play the parts of members of a committee of the state legislature. You will participate in a scripted debate on proposed legislation regulating the Right to Refuse Medical Treatment.

TASK 2: "Statutory Drafting."

Working collaboratively, the entire team is now charged with drafting a statute that will pass constitutional muster that will govern a patient's right to refuse life-saving medical treatment when there is a substituted surrogate. The primary objective is to anticipate and ensure that the proposed legislation will withstand a constitutional challenge in federal court.

PARTICIPANTS NEEDED:

Task 1 is a collaborative project; 2 to 3 students should participate

Task 2 is a collaborative project; 2 to 3 students should participate

ESTIMATED TIME FOR COMPLETION:

Task 1: 45 minutes

Task 2: 1 hour

LEVEL OF DIFFICULTY (1 to 5):

Task 1:

Task 2:

ROLE IN EXERCISE: You and your colleagues are acting as members of a committee of the state legislature. You are considering legislation regarding a patient's right to refuse life-sustaining medical treatment through the substituted judgment of a surrogate decision-maker. You will present each side in the debate. A third student will also participate as a tie-breaker. You will then collaborate and draft a statute that will withstand constitutional scrutiny. Before you begin the tasks, read the accompanying newspaper article provided on the next page for background on the issue. You might also want to read the resources listed below for a more in-depth understanding of the topic.

Battle Over Nashville Woman's Fate Intensifies

By Carlyn Ross, Staff Reporter
NASHVILLE, Tenn. –

After more than 18 months of intense and emotional battles, a Nashville family remains divided over the fate of Marjan Munoz. The 32-year-old middle school music teacher has been in a persistent vegetative state following a New Year's Eve car accident that left her in a coma. Her parents, Carol Reyes and Helena Carr, have been begging court officials and hospital administrators to maintain the life-support measures sustaining Ms. Munoz. Meanwhile, Marjan Munoz's husband, Michael Munoz, wants her life-support measures removed.

"This is my decision, and I don't know why her parents are making this more difficult than it already is," said Michael Munoz, who married Marjan 8 years ago. "If I could, I would make this all go away, but no one should suffer the way she has been suffering."

Michael Munoz, who visits his wife at the hospital at least four times a week, says his wife had never expressed conclusively whether she wished to end life-support measures in the event of a crisis. He acknowledged that Marjan Munoz had no living will, but stressed that she was an avid cyclist, dancer and musician who embraced an active lifestyle. Said Michael Munoz: "It is hard to imagine that she would want to live the rest of her life in such a sad state. This is just a shell of the life she imagined for herself."

Carol Reyes and Helena Carr, however, are convinced that their only child would want otherwise.

"She is a fighter," said Reyes. "She always has been a warrior. We visit her every day and I know she understands we are there for her." Reyes also alluded to the family's faith in God and belief in everyday miracles. "Our faith will pull us through," she said. "We have not given up. We never will."

Doctors have almost uniformly characterized Marjan Munoz's injuries as those with extensive and irreversible brain injury. Marjan Munoz has been the subject of more than a dozen neurological exams, each yielding the same result. She is dependent on feeding tubes for life.

In addition to the division among her family members, Marjan Munoz's case has also ignited community concern. On one end of the spectrum are advocates who want to continue life-sustaining measures. Groups such as "Not Dead Yet" — a disability-rights group dedicated to end-of-life issues — work to protect the lives of people facing debilitating illnesses and injuries. On the other extreme, groups such as "Die with Dignity" promote the rights of people with terminal or extreme illnesses to end their lives. The parking lot of Marjan Munoz's hospital is frequently marked by protestors from both camps.

Tennessee lawmakers are expected to consider legislation on this issue in its upcoming session. Though the state has guidelines regulating living wills already in place, there are currently no provisions regarding the necessary standards hospitals may impose for accepting the judgment of a surrogate decision-maker. The state of Tennessee has been paying for the cost of Marjan Mundy's hospitalization.

TASK 1: The Great Debate: Assessing the Strengths and Weaknesses of an Issue.

Your team will play the parts of members of the Tennessee state legislature. Each team member has been assigned a "Starter Script" that will direct his or her role in the debates leading up to drafting a "Right to Die" bill. The legislature is crafting the bill in response to a media frenzy connected to Michael Munoz, his wife Marjan Munoz, and her parents, Carol Reyes and Helena Carr. (Read the article attached here for your background information about the ordeal.) Your first task is to consider the strengths and weaknesses of your arguments, measure each point against existing case law on the issue and craft "talking points" for your position. You will then participate in a debate. One student will serve as the moderator and tie-breaker. To get you started on your debate, "Starter Scripts" have been provided for members of your team. Speakers should confine themselves to constitutional arguments. The suggested time limit for each speaker is 10 minutes. You are also encouraged to record your debates for critique.

Speaker 1:

You are an active member of the Hemlock Society, which would advocate the legalization of assisted suicide. Following the death of your father four years ago after a long, painful battle with a serious illness, you became fiercely committed to helping people end their lives with dignity. You tried to sponsor a bill for assisted suicide last year, but it never got out of committee. This year, you are advocating a bill that would protect a patient's right to refuse medical treatment in the event a substituted surrogate is needed. You are concerned that this will not pass constitutional review.

Speaker 2:

You are a firm believer in the absolute sanctity of human life. Your beliefs are rooted in your experiences as a religious fundamentalist who believes that human life should be preserved at all costs; you are categorically opposed to allowing anyone to refuse any medical treatment at any time. In the past, you have lobbied hard against suicide bills, euthanasia, assisted suicide and the refusal of any medical treatment. You believe that saving human life is too important to delegate this decision to anyone. You failed in the past in your efforts to block Tennessee legislation that allows a person to withdraw life-support measures in advance (such as through a "living will"). However, you are now determined to block the bill being proposed that would allow a patient to refuse life-saving medical treatment through the judgment of a surrogate.

Moderator/Tie-breaker:

You will hear both arguments and evaluate the speakers with the score sheet provided. Each speaker should be given 10 minutes for an argument. Feel free to prompt with questions if you believe this will be helpful to the discussion. Vote with one or the other side of this debate, or perhaps more realistically, offer some compromise based on your own personal views, beliefs and understanding of the Constitution.

TASK 2: Statutory Drafting.

Draft a statute so that it complies with the Supreme Court precedent concerning the right to refuse medical treatment, including the life-sustaining hydration and nutrition measures, through the substituted judgment of a surrogate decision-maker. Among the issues that must be considered in drafting the document are: the weight of oral testimony in supporting the client's wishes to avoid unwanted medical treatment, what a state can require as evidence that a person wants treatment terminated and, possibly, the ability of a competent person to make an advance designation of a surrogate or guardian to make a subsequent decision on life-saving treatment.

APPENDIX A

Legislative Debate Score Sheet

Judge: Speaker:	CIRCLE ONE: Speaker 1/ Speaker 2
Substance *(maximum 5 points)* • Demonstrates familiarity with the facts • Demonstrates understanding of the legal issues presented in this case • Demonstrates knowledge of the applicable legal principles	
Effectiveness *(maximum 5 points)* • Makes clear, concise points about the applicable law and provides authority supporting those points • Effectively analogizes to and distinguishes from other cases (either prompted or unprompted) • Effectively rebuts adversary's points, implicitly or explicitly	
Organization *(maximum 5 points)* • Uses strong, direct introduction, persuasive statement of the issues, and compelling "theme" • Keeps presentation of facts concise and focused • Emphasizes most important issues • Effectively manages time; does not exceed allotted time limit	
Forensic Performance *(maximum 5 points)* • Demeanor — good eye contact, posture, and body language; tone is conversational but not too informal • Speech — volume, clarity, inflection, pace; minimizes "uh" and "um" • Courtesy — respectful, non-antagonistic	
Winner **TOTAL (20 max) POINTS:**	

COMMENTS/NOTES:

———

Resources: Additional resources are available on the **LexisNexis Web Course** that was created for this book.

Chapter 9

EQUAL PROTECTION

INTRODUCTION

The Equal Protection Clause of the 14th Amendment provides "[n]o state shall . . . deny to any person within its jurisdiction the equal protection of the laws." The Equal Protection Clause strives to ensure that similarly-situated people are treated similarly. Though textually limited to states, the Supreme Court held in *Bolling v. Sharpe*, 347 U.S. 497 (1954), that the constitutional norm of equality also applies to the federal government through the Due Process Clause of the Fifth Amendment.[1]

In its Equal Protection jurisprudence, the Supreme Court evaluates claims based on the classification in the challenged law. When evaluating an Equal Protection question, the Court's primary consideration is whether the classification enacted by the government is justified by a sufficient purpose. Professor Erwin Chemerinsky has reduced Equal Protection analysis to three essential inquiries: 1) What is the classification? 2) What is the appropriate level of scrutiny? and 3) Does the government action meet the level of scrutiny?[2] These three basic questions must be considered when conducting an Equal Protection analysis.

At the onset, it is important to note that there are two ways that laws can classify. First, laws can make distinctions among people based on the plain language of the law, i.e., on the face of the statute. A state law that requires student drivers to be at least 15 years old, for instance, makes a facial distinction between those who are old enough to qualify as a student driver (15 year olds) and those who are not (those under 15). Therefore, such a law would be considered facially discriminatory because it is discriminatory in its means. Alternatively, some laws are facially neutral and appear to apply to all people equally; however, some laws may have a discriminatory impact or effect in their administration. Such laws would be considered facially neutral but are discriminatory in its ends. For example, a local law that requires all firefighters to be at least six feet tall will have a discriminatory impact on women because more men than women can satisfy this requirement. The discriminatory impact or administrative consequence alone, however, is never enough to prove a suspect or quasi-suspect classification. Instead, the Court also requires proof of a purpose or intent on the part of the government to discriminate. Several considerations are examined to prove discriminatory intent, which is a question of fact considering all the circumstances of the case. These factors, announced in *Village of Arlington Heights v. Metropolitan Housing Development Corp.*, 429 U.S. 252 (1977),

---

[1] Bolling v. Sharpe, 347 U.S. 497, 500 (1954).

[2] *See* Erwin Chemerinsky, Constitutional Law 718-22 (3d ed. 2009).

include: 1) historical background of the decision; 2) events leading up to the challenged decision; 3) departure from normal procedural sequence; 4) substantive departures; and 5) the legislative or administrative history.[3] Considering the evidence provided in the context of the foregoing factors, a court may determine that a discriminatory intent is present and find that the plaintiffs have established their prima facie case. Even if the plaintiffs have made out a prima facie case, however, the burden shifts to the government to prove that there was some neutral, non-invidious purpose for the policy being challenged.

Depending on the type of classification applied by the government, the level of review applied by the court will vary. Classifications are typically subject to three different levels of judicial scrutiny and the level of scrutiny is the test that is applied to determine if the law is unconstitutional. For instance, suspect classifications based on Race, Alienage or National Origin receive the most stringent level of scrutiny — strict scrutiny — and generally require that the state meet its burden of showing that the challenged law is necessarily related to a compelling state interest. This level of scrutiny is a difficult standard to meet, and was once described as "strict in theory and fatal in fact" by Professor Gerald Gunther. Alienage classifications, however, are only sometimes subject to strict scrutiny. When the federal government classifies on the basis of alienage, the legislation is subject to low level rational basis review (see discussion below). Furthermore, state regulations that involve political or governmental functions are also subject to rational basis review.

The second level of scrutiny applies when the law makes a classification based on gender or status as a non-marital child, the law must be substantially related to an important state interest. In both instances, the state has the burden of proof.

Finally, a third level of scrutiny is reserved for laws that distinguish on every other basis. Such rational basis classifications could be based on age, wealth, or any other policy basis for making a distinction. Classifications subject to this lowest level of scrutiny are upheld as long as they are rationally related to a legitimate state interest. Indeed, rational level review is so deferential that it amounts to a formula for upholding legislation.

The challenger bears the burden of proof in challenging such legislation. In cases subject to the rational basis test, high deference is given to the legislature. Only plainly arbitrary, capricious, and irrational laws will fail such a challenge. The Supreme Court has, however, held that animus toward a particular group of people cannot survive a rational basis test. In *Romer v. Evans*, 517 U.S. 620 (1996), the Court struck down a Colorado amendment that prevented local lawmakers from enacting laws that banned discrimination based on sexual orientation.[4] Because the Court seems willing to use more exacting scrutiny when a law is supposedly subject to rational basis review, the test has been dubbed "rational basis with a bite." (The test

---

[3] Village of Arlington Heights v. Metro. Hous. Dev. Corp., 429 U.S. 252, 253 (1977).

[4] *See also* City of Cleburne, Tex. v. Cleburne Living Ctr. Inc., 473 US 432, 450 (1985) (Invalidating a city ordinance that required a special permit for mentally retarded individuals to live together. Holding that such a permit rests "on an irrational prejudice against the mentally retarded . . . .").

may also suggest that animus against a particular class of people is, on its face, irrational.)

EXERCISE 9.1: FIRE AND VICE

SUBSTANTIVE CONTENT:

- Introduction to the 14th Amendment's Equal Protection Clause

- Requirement for discriminatory intent and discriminatory impact for facially neutral laws

- Determination of ways in which discriminatory intent can be proven

- Levels of scrutiny

SKILLS AND VALUES UTILIZED:

- Fact analysis and development

- Creative problem solving

- Judgments about outcome determinative facts

- Collaborative problem solving

- Introduction to fact-gathering tool of deposition

- Communication skills

- Review of the Federal Rules of Civil Procedure that govern depositions

GENERAL DESCRIPTION OF EXERCISE:

Drafting questions for a deposition, playing the role of attorney, deponent and the attorney defending a deposition and reviewing the federal rules governing a deposition. This exercise requires four participants.

PARTICIPANTS NEEDED:

Task 1 is an individual project.

Task 2 is a collaborative project, involving four students.

ESTIMATED TIME FOR COMPLETION:

Task 1: 1 hour

Task 2: One-half hour to prepare and two hours for your group to meet and discuss and then summarize the discussion for the entire class, if required by professor.

LEVEL OF DIFFICULTY (1 to 5):

Task 1:

Task 2:

ROLE IN EXERCISE:

TASK 1: Deposition Preparation.

Your job here is to prepare questions for a deposition to be used in a case your client, Carlos Alvarez, has filed suit against the City of Chicago. He has filed a lawsuit against the city's fire department alleging an Equal Protection violation.

TASK 2: Deposition Simulation.

You will still be in the role of attorney for Mr. Carlos Alvarez. However, three other people will be needed to complete the activity. The other parts will include: the attorney for the City of Chicago, a city commissioner responsible for passing Exam Eighty and a "reporter" who will observe the deposition.

TASK 1: Deposition Preparation.

Mr. Alvarez, a Cuban immigrant, has applied for a job with the City of Chicago to work as a firefighter. His life-long dream is to be a firefighter, and he has completed all of the necessary training. He has also successfully completed the physical portion of the screening process. As a final part of the application process, the city requires all applicants to complete a writing exam. The exam, known as "Exam Eighty," tests applicants on their writing,, spelling, and basic grammar skills. The city council, which instituted the exam five years ago, has maintained in past commission meetings that Exam Eighty is needed to spare the city from embarrassing public records written by and released by members of the fire department. All hires are required to earn a score of 80 percent or better on the 200-question exam.

An on-line news source revealed in a story last month that the city's fire department is disproportionately staffed by white employees. Furthermore, the article cited some shocking statistics related to the applicant and hiring yield for the city's fire department: For the past five years, of the 200+ applicants for a position on the fire department, only 3 percent were filled by minorities. Of the 5 percent of minorities hired by the department only 2 percent identified themselves as Hispanic. (The City of Chicago recently reported a Hispanic population of 26 percent.) Furthermore, Hispanics tested by the city's fire department are twice as likely to fail Exam Eighty as their white counterparts.

Mr. Alvarez, who came to this country with his father when he was six years old and has lived in the United States for the past nineteen years, only scored a 72 percent on Exam Eighty. His application with the city's fire department was therefore rejected. He is convinced that Exam Eighty discriminates against him and other Hispanics.

You are challenged here with compiling questions for the deposition scheduled in a week with Sam Johnson, one of the five city commissioners serving on Chicago's commission. You should carefully draft questions that will help you develop information regarding your client's Equal Protection challenge.[5] Specifically, you are limited in this phase of your discovery to developing more facts to demonstrate that the city exhibited a discriminatory intent or purpose in implementing the requirement for Exam Eighty. Mr. Alvarez has already told you that in his conversations with other city employees he has learned that the City of Chicago made some radical departures from "business as usual" in passing the exam requirement at its meeting on March 15, 2012. You need to develop these facts in the deposition with Commissioner Johnson.

First, develop a list of helpful information that you hope the deponent will provide. In an effort to illicit the most helpful evidence from the witness, first draft an outline of the information you need to obtain from a deposition. Then, draft at least three questions for each of the avenues you wish to explore. Remember to ask the most important question — "why?" — when the deponent testifies to doing or saying something. Also, remember that *Village of Arlington Heights* provides you with important considerations to prove discriminatory intent that you might want to incorporate when drafting your questions.

To get you started a sample from the outline and some correlating questions are crafted for you below.

Outline for Deposition	Questions for Deponent
⇒ **Procedural Departures**	1. How many public hearings are usually held before the city imposes new job requirements? 2. Did the city hold the regularly scheduled public hearings on Exam Eighty? 3. Why or why not?

TASK 2: Deposition Simulation.

This is a role play activity for four people. You will still be in the role of attorney for Mr. Carlos Alvarez. However, three other people will be needed to complete the activity. A second person will function as the attorney for the City of Chicago. Another

---

[5] A broader issue here is a concern about how far your client can actually go into inquiring about the motivation behind decisions from the city council. *See Village of Arlington Heights*, 429 U.S. 252. The Supreme Court has expressed a reluctance to allow the "substantial intrusion" of judicial inquiries (prodded by litigants) "into the workings of" the legislative or executive branch. *Id.* at 268 n.18.

will play the role of Mr. Sam Johnson, one of the city commissioners responsible for passing Exam Eighty. Finally, the fourth member of the group will be the "reporter" who will observe the deposition and take notes offering a critique of how well the deposition simulation aligns with the federal rules.

Taking the questions that were drafted in Task 1, have the attorney for Mr. Alvarez conduct his or her best deposition of Mr. Sam Johnson, one of the City of Chicago Commissioners responsible for passing Exam Eighty. At the same time, a third student will play the role of Ms. Sonali Patel, the attorney for the City of Chicago. The fourth student will function as an "observer" who will monitor the deposition and keep the players on track.

Write questions and answers. Record or ask someone to function as "reporter." Examine the questions you developed in Task 1. Now with another student or students, consider the questions against the outline that was prepared. Are there any questions you will consider asking at the end of your deposition? Working in teams of two or three, make your best effort at staging a deposition. One student can play the attorney for Mr. Alvarez, another can play Commissioner Anderson and the third can play the role of the city attorney.

CRITIQUE SHEET FOR TASK 2: DEPOSITION SIMULATION

Attorney for Mr. Carlos Alvarez Played By: _____

City Attorney Played By: _____

Mr. Sam Johnson Played By: _____

Before the deposition begins, remind all of the participants of their respective goals in the simulation. Also pay close attention to whether the questions asked and answered reveal a discriminatory intent by the City of Chicago. Once the simulation has started, use this critique sheet to help guide you through your review.

1. According to the attorney representing Mr. Carlos Alvarez, what are the constitutional defects inherent in the "Exam Eighty"? Were the attorney's questions on this issue thorough enough to expose this assertion? What would you add?

2. Based on the answers supplied by Mr. Sam Johnson, what type of defense might the city raise?

3. If you were serving as the city attorney, which questions would you ask? Why?

4. Does any single question have the potential to reveal a "smoking gun" that would seal the case? Why or why not?

5. Which of the players involved faced the greatest challenge? Why?

Name of Observer: _____

Chapter 10

PRIVILEGES OR IMMUNITIES CLAUSE

INTRODUCTION

The Privileges or Immunities Clause of the Fourteenth Amendment should be distinguished from the Privileges and Immunities Clause of Article IV. The latter is essentially a comity clause that prevents states from imposing discriminatory regulations on out-of-staters with respect to a constitutional right or an important economic activity. Most of these challenges under Article IV's Privileges and Immunities Clause involve the right to earn a living.

The Privileges or Immunities Clause of the Fourteenth Amendment was practically eviscerated by the *Slaughter-House Cases*. In *Slaughter-House Cases Butchers' Benevolent Assn. of New Orleans v. Crescent City Livestock Landing & Slaughter-House Co.*, 83 U.S. (16 Wall.) 36 (1873), the Court specifically refused to apply the Privileges or Immunities Clause as a basis for invalidating state and local laws. Instead, the Court held at the time that the Privileges or Immunities of citizenship were "left to the State governments for security and protection . . . ."[1] The narrow interpretation of the 14th Amendment's Privileges or Immunities Clause has generally remained in place.

However, *Saenz v. Roe*, 526 U.S. 489 (1999), resuscitated the Privileges or Immunities Clause as a basis for invalidating laws that impair the exercise of uniquely federal rights. These rights include the right of a United States citizen who establishes residency in one state to be treated similarly to long-time residents of the same state. At least in a limited capacity, the Privileges or Immunities Clause was used to protect the right to travel; specifically, the clause guarded against the burdens of durational residency requirements. In *Saenz*, discrimination against the newly arrived residents was the basis for the Court's use of the 14th Amendment's Privileges or Immunities Clause to strike a state law. The Court considered interstate movement a fundamental right and found a "constitutional right to travel from one State to another."[2]

---

[1] Butchers Benevolent Ass'n of New Orleans v. Crescent City Livestock Landing & Slaughter House Co., 83 U.S. (16 Wall.) 36, 78–79 (1873).

[2] Saenz v. Roe, 526 U.S. 489, 498 (1999) (quoting United States v. Guest, 383 U.S. 745, 757 (1966)).

EXERCISE 10.1: FAMILY MATTERS

SUBSTANTIVE CONTENT:

- Introduction to Privileges or Immunities Clause of 14th Amendment
- Explanation of Right to Travel
- Introduction to Model Rules governing Pro Bono Service

SKILLS AND VALUE UTILIZED:

- Integration of law and fact
- Doctrinal knowledge
- Problem-solving
- Drafting a demand letter
- Drafting a complaint

GENERAL DESCRIPTION OF EXERCISE:

TASK 1: Writing a Letter of Appeal.

You have taken on a case *pro bono* to write a letter of appeal on behalf of a family that has been stripped of temporary financial assistance by the state.

TASK 2: Drafting a Complaint.

You are representing the same family from Task 1 *pro bono*, and you have proceeded to draft a complaint on their behalf challenging the denial of financial assistance provided by the State of Georgia.

Participants Needed:

Task 1 is an individual project.

Task 2 is an individual project.

ESTIMATED TIME FOR COMPLETION:

Task 1: 1 hour

Task 2: Three hours

LEVEL OF DIFFICULTY (1 to 5):

Task 1:

Task 2:

ROLE IN EXERCISE: You are acting as a new associate at a small family law firm in Georgia. Your role here is to help the Weavers challenge the state's denial of temporary assistance. You begin by writing a letter of appeal to the state. After all of the required administrative remedies have been exhausted, you are asked to draft a complaint challenging the denial of benefits. The complaint will be filed in the United State District Court for the Northern District of Georgia.

TASK 1: Writing a Letter of Appeal.

After a hurricane strikes Florida and destroys their mobile home, the Weaver family (Jay, Julie, and their two young children) relocate to Atlanta, Georgia. After almost three weeks of struggling to find employment in the state, Jay and Julie Weaver decide to apply for Temporary Assistance for Families in Need from the State of Georgia. The parents have no other options to feed their two children. After completing the necessary paperwork, the Weavers submit their application for aid. After a week, they receive a letter of denial from the state.

A copy of the letter is attached below:

The State of Georgia

Administrative Complex, 24435 Peachtree Drive SE, Atlanta, Georgia, 30353.
404.555.1212

Mr. Jay Weaver & Ms. Julie Weaver
1480 MLK Drive
Atlanta, Ga. 30353

NOTICE OF DENIAL

August 5, 2012

Dear Sir/Madam:

The State of Georgia's Office of Temporary Financial Assistance for Families in
Need is responsible for distributing assistance to families. After reviewing your
application, this office has denied your application for assistance.

Under state law, you do not meet the requirements for the program. Official
Georgia Code § 375 precludes a disbursement to you at this time.

If you dispute our determination of your ineligibility, you may appeal this
decision by writing to this office within 30 days of receipt of this letter.

Sincerely,

Jeffrey Glenn

Senior Administrator

　　Distraught about their inability to meet their basic needs, the Weavers have come
to you for assistance. You are a new associate in a small family law practice. Your firm
has agreed to represent the Weavers on a *pro bono* basis.

　　Though you are working for the Weavers in a *pro bono* capacity, remember that the
American Bar Association ("ABA") Rules on *pro bono* service govern your conduct.
Here is an excerpt of the relevant section of the ABA Rules on *pro bono* service:

Rule 6.1 Voluntary Pro Bono Publico Service

Every lawyer has a professional responsibility to provide legal services to those unable to pay. A lawyer should aspire to render at least (50) hours of pro bono publico legal services per year. In fulfilling this responsibility, the lawyer should:

(a) provide a substantial majority of the (50) hours of legal services without fee or expectation of fee to:

(1) persons of limited means or

(2) charitable, religious, civic, community, governmental and educational organizations in matters that are designed primarily to address the needs of persons of limited means; and

(b) provide any additional services through:

(1) delivery of legal services at no fee or substantially reduced fee to individuals, groups or organizations seeking to secure or protect civil rights, civil liberties or public rights, or charitable, religious, civic, community, governmental and educational organizations in matters in furtherance of their organizational purposes, where the payment of standard legal fees would significantly deplete the organization's economic resources or would be otherwise inappropriate;

(2) delivery of legal services at a substantially reduced fee to persons of limited means; or

(3) participation in activities for improving the law, the legal system or the legal profession.

In addition, a lawyer should voluntarily contribute financial support to organizations that provide legal services to persons of limited means.

Please draft a one page letter to the State of Georgia appealing the denial of benefits. Make a constitutional challenge to the statute. A copy of the statute is attached here for your review:

OFFICIAL GEORGIA CODE § 375

Eligibility to receive benefits under the Temporary Aid for Families in Need

1. Recipients (with few exceptions) must work as soon as they are job ready or no later than two years after coming on assistance.

2. Single parents are required to participate in work activities for at least 30 hours per week. Two-parent families must participate in work activities 35 or 55 hours a week, depending upon circumstances.

3. Failure to participate in work requirements can result in a reduction or termination of benefits to the family.

4. Recipients must establish residency in the state of Georgia at least 12 months prior to the application for benefits.

TASK 2: Drafting a Complaint.

Despite your best efforts to have the state reinstate the temporary financial assistance through your letter of appeal, the State of Georgia has denied your request. Still unable to pay for basic living expenses, the Weavers have asked you to file a lawsuit on their behalf. You should now draft a complaint challenging the state's denial of benefits; specifically, you are challenging the application of a durational residency requirement in connection with temporary assistance. The complaint will challenge the state's conduct as a violation of the Weaver's rights under the 14th Amendment's Privileges or Immunities Clause. The complaint must track the law announced in relevant Supreme Court case law. It must also include all legally relevant facts.

Remember to draft your complaint challenging the state's conduct against the backdrop of Sovereign Immunity principles. Therefore, make sure you identify the proper defendant in the lawsuit. At this point, you may want to review *Ex Parte Young* for a discussion of the stripping doctrine.

In drafting a complaint, attorneys may use many resources and are bound by several filing rules. The local court rules for the receiving court apply. Part of this activity may require you to locate and review the local court rules for the Northern District of Georgia. (Speak to your professor about whether you need to take this extra step.)

Complaints commence legal actions and provide notice to defendants. In general, the complaint outlines the scope of the lawsuit. It is written in point form with numbered allegations. The essential elements of a complaint filed in federal court include the following:[3]

1.   Name of court

2.   Names of all plaintiffs

3.   Names of all defendants

4.   Title of document

5.   Civil Action Number (to be assigned by the court)

6.   Statement of court's jurisdiction

7.   Statement of court's venue

8.   List of parties

9.   Facts (must be stated clearly enough to satisfy the elements of the claim)

10.   Statement of legal claims

---

[3] Local Court Rules may also expand the essential elements of a complaint. Check the rules for your court.

11. Demand

12. Signature

13. Date

Resources: Additional resources are available on the **LexisNexis Web Course** that was created for this book.

Chapter 11

THE PROTECTION OF ECONOMIC RIGHTS

INTRODUCTION

There are various protections in the Constitution and its Amendments affording protection of economic rights. The Contract Clause, Article I, Section 10, protects individuals against retroactive government impairment of contracts, including contracts between private parties and contracts between the government and private parties. Other important economic protections exist. The Due Process Clauses of the Fifth Amendment and Fourteenth Amendment both protect against unreasonable laws, including those relating to commerce. At one time, during the so-called *Lochner* era in the early 1900s, due process also was used to protect the substantive value of free markets from government incursions through what became known as substantive due process. The dormant Commerce Clause, through Article I, Section 8, limits state and local governments from discriminating against or placing an undue burden on interstate commerce. Last but not least, the Takings Clause of the Fifth Amendment provides that government can take private property for public use, but must pay just compensation if it does so.

The problem in this chapter is about the Contract Clause. As set forth in Article I, Section 10, the Contract Clause prohibits states from enacting any "Law impairing the Obligation of Contracts" and serves as a limitation on state exercise of police powers. The Clause specifically applies to existing and not prospective contracts.

The Contract Clause served as a significant state limitation in the early 1800s. In *Fletcher v. Peck*, 10 U.S. (6 Cranch) 87 (1810), a unanimous Court overturned the Georgia legislature's rescission of a land grant that had been tainted by bribery and fraud. The legislature's rescission was challenged by persons who acquired land in the aftermarket. The buyers claimed they were purchasers in due course and that the land was now theirs. The Court found that the legislature could not annul a land grant or contract by overturning a valid law and penalizing bona fide purchasers. *See also Dartmouth College v. Woodward*, 17 U.S. (4 Wheat) 518 (1819) (where the Court struck down New Hampshire's effort to alter the College's charter in an effort to change the composition of the College's Board).

Modern interpretation of Contract Clause limits have been generally narrower than in earlier eras, but not without force. The Contract Clause does not flatly prohibit all retroactive legislative contract impairment. Based on Supreme Court interpretations, the Clause permits retroactive impairment of contracts depending on the context. To trigger Contract Clause analysis, there must be a substantial impairment of a contract, meaning a significant enervation of a party's rights pursuant to the contract. If there is substantial impairment of a private contract, the law must be reasonable and serve a legitimate and important public interest, essentially a form of intermediate scrutiny, and be reasonably and narrowly tailored to advancing that interest. If the law retroactively impaired a government contract, the Clause triggered an even closer scrutiny.

In *Home Building & Loan Assn. v. Blaisdell*, 290 U.S. 398 (1934), a case decided during the Great Depression, the Court considered the validity of a mortgage moratorium law in the state of Minnesota. The Act provided mortgage relief to mortgagors while the economic emergency existed, postponing foreclosures and other judicial proceedings. The Court observed that the Contract Clause is "not an absolute" and need not be read literally. Consequently, the Court found that the law was reasonable under the circumstances, particularly in light of its temporary nature, and that it did not violate the Contract Clause.

In another case involving a Minnesota law, *Allied Structural Steel v. Spannaus*, 438 U.S. 234 (1978), the Supreme Court considered modifications of contracts to which the government was a party. The Court struck down an application of Minnesota's Private Pension Benefits Protection Act, effectively applying a higher standard for meeting Contract Clause requirements than for government modifications of private contracts. The Court found that if there was a substantial impairment of a contract to which a state was a party, the modification had to be both necessary and reasonable, citing *United States Trust Co. v. New Jersey*, 431 U.S. 1 (1977).

EXERCISE 11.1: THE PURPLE PENSION PLAN

SKILLS AND VALUES UTILIZED:

- Issue Identification and organization.

- Concise statement of important issues.

ESTIMATED TIME FOR COMPLETION: 1 hour

LEVEL OF DIFFICULTY (1 to 5):

ROLE IN EXERCISE: You are an attorney for the public employees union in the State of Shock.

BACKGROUND INFORMATION: The State of Shock is a small western state known for its independence and great government job benefits, particularly a wonderful pension plan set forth in Chapter 4A of the State Code. In some states, the pension plans are included in the state constitutions or are a part of a collective bargaining process between a union and the state. The structure is different in Shock, which has a unique legislative foundation for its pensions. In the year 1960, state workers in Shock could retire at the age of 60 with a pension of approximately 50% of their last year's working salary, without any cost-of-living adjustments. By the year 2000, the retirement age was lowered to 50, with a maximum pension of 80% of the last year's working salary. Annual cost-of-living increases also were guaranteed, determined by federal governmental indices. With raises, the subsequent payments could exceed 100% of the last year's working salary. By the year 2008, the unfunded pension liability of Shock was estimated to be around $7 billion, almost equivalent to the state's annual budget. In 2009, two small towns in Shock declared bankruptcy because the unfunded municipal pensions were almost $100 million in debt and without any viable way of recouping the money.

The state legislature considers enacting a new bill, the State Employee Retirement Security Act, that would substantially modify Chapter 4A, the state pension plan. Specifically, the proposed law would do the following:

1. Eliminate all cost-of-living increases for the next decade at a minimum for current and future retirees.

2. Raise the retirement age prospectively to at least 65 for all future retirees.

3. Change the nature of the payouts to a combination of fixed-income and stock/bond option plan like a 401(k) for future retirees.

4. Apply to current retirees to reduce their payout if the underfunding of the plan sinks past a stated level determined to be dangerous for the fiscal health of the

state.

EXERCISE: As an attorney for the predominant labor union in Shock that represents service employees, including more than 1,000 state government employees, you are asked to review the law and do the following:

1.   Write a thesis statement, describing the union position in five or six sentences, to be read by the labor union's president to the media later that day.

2.   Prepare testimony to be given by the president of the union to a committee of the state legislature the following week. A sympathetic legislator will be asking the questions and has asked for an outline of questions that would help build the union's cause. (The legislator said she turned purple with rage when she heard about the proposed law.) The testimony should include at least seven questions and answers.

Chapter 12

THE FREEDOM OF SPEECH

A. PRIOR RESTRAINTS

INTRODUCTION

Prior restraints occur at the intersection of the Free Press Clause and the Free Speech Clause. Justice Holmes went through an early decisional phase when he interpreted the First Amendment narrowly to amount only to a prohibition on government restraints prior to publication. This view was based on the pernicious history of English licensing laws, which set John Milton's teeth on edge in his famous polemic *Areopagitica* and which later were singled out for common law opprobrium by Blackstone in his influential *Commentaries*. *See Schenck v. United States*, 249 U.S. 47, 51-52 (1919). Two Supreme Court cases incorporated that historical skepticism and philosophical disapproval into the doctrine of the First Amendment.

* * *

In *Near v. Minnesota*, 283 U.S. 697 (1931), the Supreme Court struck down a state statute that permitted a court to "perpetually enjoin" as a nuisance any "malicious, scandalous and defamatory newspaper, magazine or other periodical." Once enjoined, the newspaper was subject to the state court's contempt power. Chief Justice Hughes easily ruled: "This is of the essence of censorship." *Id.* at 713. Prior restraints thus became understood to be the most serious and least tolerable infringement on First Amendment rights. A civil sanction or criminal punishment subsequent to the speech manifests the harm of *chilling* speech — speakers are deterred from speaking. By comparison, a prior restraint is immediate and irreversible, and has the most severe possible effect on public discourse to altogether prevent the speech from being spoken or published in the first place — it *freezes* the speech. *See Nebraska Press Ass'n v. Stuart*, 427 U.S. 539, 559 (1976). For this reason, the Supreme Court has declared, "Any system of prior restraints of expression comes to this Court bearing a heavy presumption against its constitutional validity." *Bantam Books, Inc. v. Sullivan*, 372 U.S. 58, 70 (1963).

Those principles were applied to the serious problem of national security in a canonical decision which is found in nearly every constitutional law casebook and is famously known as *The Pentagon Papers Case. New York Times Co. v. United States*, 403 U.S. 713 (1971). If it were reduced to a bumper sticker, however, the slogan could read: "Great Case/Little Law."

In two separate proceedings, the United States had sought to enjoin a newspaper from publishing a classified government study of our military involvement and policies in Vietnam. In both cases, the district court refused to grant an injunction. The government won an appeal in the Second Circuit against the respondent *New York Times*; the government lost an appeal in the D.C. Circuit against the respondent *Washington Post*. Suggesting the importance and unusualness of the issues, the Supreme Court set the case for briefing and oral argument three days later and then issued its decision only four days after argument. That procedural celerity and deep philosophical differences among the individual justices resulted in a set of opinions that shed more heat than light on the issue. Without any further elaboration, a lowest common denominator *per curiam* opinion succinctly declared the obvious:

> "Any system of prior restraints of expression comes to this Court bearing a heavy presumption against its constitutional validity." The Government "thus carries a heavy burden of showing justification for the imposition of such a restraint." The District Court for the Southern District of New York in the *New York Times* case and the District Court for the District of Columbia and the Court of Appeals for the District of Columbia Circuit, in the *Washington Post* case held that the Government had not met that burden. We agree.

New York Times, 403 U.S. at 714 (citations omitted).

The separate opinions in the case can be grouped into three categories: Justices Black and Douglas maintained that a prior restraint on the press is never ever constitutional; Justices Brennan, White, Stewart, and Marshall maintained that a prior restraint on the press could be constitutional in some circumstances, but not in this case; and Chief Justice Burger and Justices Harlan and Blackmun maintained that a prior restraint on the press could be constitutional in some circumstances, and this was such a case. Overall, it was a 6-to-3 win for the newspapers. Another constitutional law take away from the justices' opinions was the 7-to-2 vote for the proposition that prior restraints were presumptively invalid but not *per se* invalid. And a majority of the justices suggested that the Executive could constitutionally obtain such an injunction either based on that branch's inherent powers alone or in conjunction with a congressional authorization. A rundown of the justices' separate opinions follows.

Justice Black took his usual principled but eccentric absolutist view: "The Government's power to censor the press was abolished so that the press would remain forever free to censure the Government." *Id.* at 717.

Justice Douglas likewise reasoned that the language of the First Amendment "leaves . . . no room for governmental restraint on the press." *Id.* at 720. He also took comfort from the fact that the government study had been distributed widely within the government and was mostly historical.

Justice Brennan rejected the government's arguments as being merely "surmise or conjecture that untoward consequences may result." The government must prove that the publication will "inevitably, directly, and immediately" result in the terrible harm. He repeated *dicta* from old cases of wartime examples of the requisite kind of harm: the actual obstruction of military recruiting or the disclosure of secret military plans such as "the sailing dates of transports or the number and location of troops." He added his own *dictum* for a peacetime example: the release of the information will "set in motion a nuclear holocaust." *Id.* at 725-27.

Justice Stewart concurred but expressed his belief that the Executive power over national defense and foreign relations could justify an injunction on a showing that disclosure would result in a "direct, immediate, and irreparable damage to our Nation or its people." *Id.* at 730.

Justice White concurred because the government had not met its "very heavy burden," although he implied that an injunction might be obtained pursuant to a statutory authorization from Congress. He also believed that the government could proceed against both newspapers and their reporters under federal criminal laws that prohibited the publication of classified information. *Id.* at 731, 737-40.

Justice Marshall based his concurrence squarely on the lack of congressional authorization for a prior restraint, and on his understanding of separation of powers. *Id.* at 745-46.

Chief Justice Burger dissented and found the injunction constitutional. He would have allowed the injunction to continue long enough to allow the courts time to hold a deliberate and orderly hearing on appeal. *Id.* at 752.

Justice Harlan complained about the undue haste in the calendaring and decision of the case. He would have upheld the injunction relying on separation of powers and the inherent power of the Executive over foreign affairs. *Id.* at 756.

Justice Blackmun was convinced that the government's grave and dire predictions were accurate and he went on to express his strong disapproval with the press and with his colleagues in the majority:

> [I]f, with the Court's action today, these newspapers proceed to publish the critical documents and there results therefrom "the death of soldiers, the destruction of alliances, the greatly increased difficulty of negotiation with our enemies, the inability of our diplomats to negotiate," to which list I might add the factors of prolongation of the war and of further delay in the freeing of United States prisoners, then the Nation's people will know where the responsibility for these sad consequences rests.

Id. at 763.

The denouement of the *Pentagon Papers Case* was that the newspapers published the excerpts of the classified government study which they had secured by an unauthorized leak from a former government employee named Daniel Ellsberg. It took years for the United States to extricate itself from the conflict in Vietnam. The government did not prosecute any of the newspapers — an option apparently left open by the justices — but it did prosecute Ellsberg. Eventually, however, the trial judge directed a verdict of acquittal for Ellsberg because of bizarre prosecution improprieties that included illegal wiretaps, the burglary of the office of his psychiatrist, and ex parte attempts to influence the trial judge. This *sui generis* case was the first and last time the Executive Branch went into federal court to seek an injunction against a newspaper prior to publication and then was willing to take the case "all the way to the Supreme Court."

EXERCISE 12.1: THE *PENTAGON PAPERS CASE* REDUX

SKILLS AND VALUES UTILIZED:

- Case analysis
- Statutory analysis
- Preparation of pleading
- Strategic thinking
- Speaking truth to power

ESTIMATED TIME FOR COMPLETION: 1 1/2 hours

LEVEL OF DIFFICULTY (1 to 5):

TASK 1: Draft a petition for a temporary restraining order.

TASK 2: Outline a briefing on the government's likelihood of success.

BACKGROUND INFORMATION: You are an attorney in the Office of Legal Counsel ("OLC") in the Department of Justice. That office provides authoritative legal advice to the President and the rest of the Executive Branch. The Assistant Attorney General in charge of OLC orders you to prepare a confidential discussion draft of a petition for a temporary restraining order against the *New York Times* ("NYT"), in response to a joint request from White House Counsel and the Counselor of the Department of State. You have been advised that your work is classified "Top Secret," i.e., the highest classification level the government reserves for matters that would compromise national security if publicly disclosed. Here is what you have been told, on a "need to know" basis, during your briefing by agents of the Federal Bureau of Investigation and the Department of Homeland Security:

- For more than a year, the NYT has been working on a story about the covert CIA program designed to sabotage the efforts of Iran to develop nuclear weapons

- Reporters in the United States and Israel have been working their sources in both governments, interviewing former American officials, European and Israeli officials, international inspectors, and outside experts

- No senior intelligence officer or current Administration official in either country has spoken to reporters "on the record," i.e., with the expectation that what they have said can be quoted and attributed to them

- Some officials who served in the Bush administration, however, have spoken with reporters "on deep background," i.e., with the expectation that the information may not be included in the article but the reporters have relied on those sources to identify other sources of information

- The FBI has reason to believe that at least one member of the Obama administration, who is under surveillance, already has provided information "not for attribution," i.e., the source's comments may be quoted but the identity of the source may not be revealed by the paper

- The NYT has learned of a secret diplomatic exchange in which Israel informed the United States of its timetable for launching a military air strike on Iran's primary complex for uranium enrichment by a date certain

- The NYT has learned that Israel requested from the United States special purpose bunker-busting bombs

- The NYT has learned that the United States refused that request temporarily but promised to reconsider its decision along Israel's timetable

- The NYT has learned that the United States also responded to Israel with increased intelligence sharing, including details of a classified CIA covert program

- The NYT has learned those shared details describing aspects of the CIA covert program of surveillance, espionage, and computer sabotage of the Iranian facility

- The NYT is preparing to publish a story sometime in the next 24 hours revealing all this information

As has been explained to you, a T.R.O. would buy needed time. The Administration wants to delay the NYT from publishing the story in order to afford senior intelligence and Administration officials the opportunity to prepare and then meet with the editors of the newspaper. The Administration hopes to convince the newspaper's editors not to reveal even the existence of the CIA covert program in order to allow it to continue to operate effectively against Iran's nuclear weapons program. Alternatively, the Administration wants to try to persuade the newspaper's editors to leave out of the stories any classified information that will compromise the CIA covert program. The Administration's additional background concern is that the story will harm foreign relations between the United States and Israel.

Your preliminary research flags two statutes.

18 U.S.C. § 798, which was referenced in some of the opinions in *The Pentagon Papers Case*, provides in part: "Whoever knowingly and willfully . . . publishes . . . any classified information . . . concerning communication intelligence activities of the United States" shall be fined or imprisoned.

18 U.S.C § 555, which recently was enacted as part of the "war on terrorism," provides:

(a) Whoever, lawfully or unlawfully, having possession of, access to, control over, or being entrusted with any information classified "top secret" pursuant to subsection (c)(1), information the unauthorized disclosure of which causes direct, immediate, and irreparable damage to the security of the United States or its citizens, or to the safety of its servicemen and servicewomen serving abroad, knowingly and willfully communicates, furnishes, transmits, publishes, or otherwise makes such information available to an unauthorized person, shall be fined under this title or imprisoned not more than ten years, or both.

(b) Whenever, in the judgment of a department or agency of the United States government expressly designated by the President pursuant to subsection (c)(1), any person has engaged or is about to engage in any acts or practices, which constitute or will constitute a violation of this section, or any regulation or order issued thereunder, the Attorney General, on behalf of the United States, may make application to the appropriate court for an order enjoining such acts or practices, or for an order enforcing compliance with such provision, and upon a showing of clear and convincing evidence by the Attorney General that such person has engaged or is about to engage in any such acts or practices, a permanent or temporary injunction, restraining order, or other order may be granted.

(c) As used in this section—

(1) The term "top secret" refers to information or material relating to the national defense that requires the highest degree of protection. Information or material is properly classified "top secret" as follows:

(A) The test for assigning "top secret" classification shall be whether its unauthorized disclosure could reasonably be expected to cause exceptionally grave damage to the national security. Examples of "exceptionally grave damage" include armed hostilities against the United States or its allies; disruption of foreign relations vitally affecting the national security; the compromise of vital national defense plans or complex cryptologic and communications intelligence systems; the revelation of sensitive intelligence operations; and the disclosure of scientific or technologic developments vital to national security. This list of examples is not exhaustive, but this classification shall be used with the utmost restraint.

(B) The authority to classify information or material "top secret" shall be restricted solely to those offices within the Executive branch that are concerned with matters of national security, and shall be limited to the minimum number absolutely required for efficient administration. The authority to classify information or material "top secret" under this section shall be exercised only by such officials as the President may designate in writing by:

(i) The heads of the Departments listed below;

(ii) Such of their senior principal duties and assistants as the heads of such Departments may designate in writing; and

(iii) Such heads and senior principal deputies and assistants of major elements of such Departments, as the heads of such Departments may designate in writing.

(iv) Such offices in the Executive Office of the President as the President may designate in writing include: Central Intelligence Agency; National Security Agency; Department of Homeland Security; Atomic Energy Commission; Department of State; Department of the Treasury; Department of Defense; Department of the Army; Department of the Navy; Department of the Air Force; United States Arms Control and Disarmament Agency; Department of Justice; National Aeronautics and Space Administration.

(2) The term "unauthorized person" means any person who, or agency which, is not authorized to receive information of the categories set forth in subsection (a) of this section, by the President, or by the head of a department or agency of the United States government which is expressly designated by the President to engage in intelligence activities for the United States.

(d) Nothing in this section shall prohibit the furnishing, upon lawful demand, of information to any regularly constituted committee of the Senate or House of Representatives of the United States of America, or joint committee thereof.

B.   RACIST SPEECH, INCITEMENTS & THREATS

INTRODUCTION

A little meta-theory comes in handy in constitutional law. John Paul Stevens — the now retired justice — once explained the foundational approach the Supreme Court takes to interpret the First Amendment. John Paul Stevens, *The Freedom of Speech*, 102 YALE L. J. 1293 (1993). The free speech clause protects "the freedom of speech;" the free speech clause does not protect all "speech." Otherwise, crimes like perjury, bribery, and blackmail which consist of speech would be immune from criminal prosecution. "[I]t has never been deemed an abridgement of freedom of speech or press to make a course of conduct illegal merely because the conduct was in part initiated, evidenced, or carried out by means of language, either spoken, written, or printed." *Giboney v. Empire Storage & Ice Co.*, 336 U.S. 490, 502 (1949). The doctrine constructed by the justices necessarily has been and continues to be "categorical," i.e., some categories of speech are protected and some categories of speech are not protected by the First Amendment . . . and the justices. (Among the protected categories of speech, it is also true that some categories are more protected than others, e.g., political speech is more protected than commercial speech. First Amendment analysis has a strict scrutiny track and an intermediate scrutiny track.)

The existing categories of speech that have been determined to be unprotected include: fighting words, *Chaplinsky v. New Hampshire*, 315 U.S. 568 (1942); threats, *Watts v. United States*, 394 U.S. 705 (1969); speech that incites imminent illegal activity, *Brandenburg v. Ohio*, 395 U.S. 444 (1969); obscenity, *Miller v. California*, 413 U.S. 15 (1973); and child pornography, *New York v. Ferber*, 458 U.S. 747 (1982). This introduction equips you to distinguish among racist speech, incitements, and threats.

Racist speech is protected speech; so-called "hate speech" is not a juridical category of speech. It is not a Supreme Court category on the list of unprotected categories and it never has been. The term appears in a Supreme Court opinion only once — casually and in a separate concurring opinion. *See R.A.V. v. City of St. Paul*, 505 U.S. 377, 401 (1992) (White, J., concurring in the judgment). Your casebook in fact includes many opinions in which the speaker has used vile racial epithets and got away with it by invoking the protection of the First Amendment. Likely, you have felt a strong opprobrium towards the speaker and a visceral disdain for the vile speech, and rightly so. But Justice Holmes believed those natural human reactions reveal the *raison d'etre* for the First Amendment: "[I]f there is any principle of the Constitution that more imperatively calls for attachment than any other it is the principle of free thought — not free thought for those who agree with us but freedom for the thought we hate." *United States v. Schwimmer*, 279 U.S. 644, 654-55 (1929). On the one hand, for decades constitutional law professors have been arguing in law review articles too numerous to count that hate speech should be added to the list of unprotected categories. On the other hand, the justices have steadfastly refused to add to the list of unprotected categories and the current justices seem to be stubbornly unwilling to do so. *See, e.g., Brown v. Entertainment Merchants Assoc.*, 131 S. Ct. 2729 (2010) (violent video games protected); *United States v. Stevens*, 130 S. Ct. 1577 (2010) (depictions of animal cruelty protected).

Most traditional constitutional law casebooks trace the long lineage of Supreme Court assessments of subversive speech and incitements to violence as an object lesson in the values underlying the freedom of speech. The selected cases showcase how great dissents by great justices, like Holmes and Brandeis, eventually came to be adopted by the Supreme Court. Let's skip over those older cases from World War I and the Red Scare and the Cold War. The modern doctrine got stuck wide open in the 1960s. In *Brandenburg v. Ohio*, 395 U.S. 444 (1969), the Supreme Court proclaimed: "These later decisions have fashioned the principle that the constitutional guarantees of free speech and free press do not permit a State to forbid or proscribe advocacy of the use of force or of law violation except where such advocacy is directed to inciting or producing imminent lawless action and is likely to incite or produce such action." *Id.* at 447. Justice Brennan, the ghostwriter of the *per curiam* opinion, came up with this test apparently because he could not come up with a test that would protect more speech of this kind. Ever since then, successful prosecutions have been *rarae aves*. *See Hess v. Indiana*, 414 U.S. 105, 108 (1973) (imminence requirement not satisfied by hollering to a crowd of demonstrators "We'll take the fucking street later!").

The unprotected category of threats is considerably more important to prosecutors today and it figures in the Exercise that follows. Two cases mark the boundaries of the category. In *R.A.V. v. City of St. Paul*, 505 U.S. 377 (1992), the Supreme Court struck down a municipal hate speech ordinance that provided: "Whoever places on public or private property a symbol, object, appellation, characterization or graffiti, including, but not limited to, a burning cross or Nazi swastika, which one knows or has reasonable grounds to know arouses anger, alarm or resentment in others on the basis of race, color, creed, religion or gender commits disorderly conduct and shall be guilty of a misdemeanor." *Id.* at 380. All nine justices voted to reverse the convictions of some cowardly and ignorant miscreants who burned a crude cross on the front lawn of their African-American neighbors in the middle of the night. The majority opinion by Justice Scalia struck down the ordinance on its face because it discriminated among categories of fighting words based on content and was underinclusive. Four justices concurred in the judgment, but rejected the First Amendment analysis in the majority opinion.

In *Virginia v. Black*, 538 U.S. 343 (2003), the plurality opinion by Justice O'Connor attempted Solomonically to cut the state statute in half: "We conclude that while a State, consistent with the First Amendment, may ban cross burning carried out with the intent to intimidate, the provision in the Virginia statute treating cross burning as prima facie evidence of intent to intimidate renders the statute unconstitutional in its current form." *Id.* at 347-48. Most significant for present purposes, the plurality explicitly defined the unprotected category:

> True threats encompass those statements where the speaker means to communicate a serious expression of an intent to commit an act of unlawful violence to a particular individual or group of individuals. The speaker need not actually intend to carry out the threat. Rather, a prohibition on true threats "protects individuals from the fear of violence" and "from the disruption that fear engenders," in addition to protecting people "from the possibility that the threatened violence will occur." Intimidation in the constitutionally proscribable sense of the word is a type of true threat, where a speaker directs a threat to a person or group of persons with the intent of placing the victim in fear of bodily harm or death.

Id. at 359-60. Thus defined, true threats describe a category of low value speech subject to government regulation, even outright prohibition and subsequent criminal punishment.

In a retro-precedent, the justices had previously explored the same boundary line between protected and unprotected speech in the particular public policy context of the Exercise that follows. In *Watts v. United States*, 394 U.S. 705 (1969), the Supreme Court reversed the defendant's conviction under 18 U.S.C. § 871(a), a statute still on the books that prohibits any person from "knowingly and willfully . . . [making] any threat to take the life of or to inflict bodily harm upon the President of the United States . . . ." The majority held that Defendant's oral statement at a peace rally on the grounds of the Washington Monument — that if he was drafted he would refuse induction into the Armed Forces — and "if they ever make me carry a rifle the first man I want in my sights is L. B. J." was merely political hyperbole and did not amount to a true threat against the life of the President of the United States. The *per curiam* opinion upheld the constitutionality of the statute, however, in only these few words:

> Certainly the statute under which [Defendant] was convicted is constitutional on its face. The Nation undoubtedly has a valid, even an overwhelming,

interest in protecting the safety of its Chief Executive and in allowing him to perform his duties without interference from threats of physical violence. Nevertheless, a statute such as this one, which makes criminal a form of pure speech, must be interpreted with the commands of the First Amendment clearly in mind. What is a threat must be distinguished from what is constitutionally protected speech.

394 U.S. at 707.

EXERCISE 12.2: PROSECUTORIAL DISCRETION: FEDERAL CRIME OR FREE SPEECH?

SKILLS AND VALUES UTILIZED:

- Statutory analysis
- Constitutional analysis
- Criminal pleading
- Strategic thinking

ESTIMATED TIME FOR COMPLETION: 1 1/2 hours

LEVEL OF DIFFICULTY (1 to 5):

TASK 1: Draft a simple federal criminal indictment based on the following facts, tracking the elements of the offense set out in the statute, in order to help you to perform Task 2.

TASK 2: Based on your review of the file and your draft indictment setting out the elements of the offense, exercise your prosecutorial best judgment to determine whether or not to bring this matter to the grand jury.

BACKGROUND INFORMATION: You are an Assistant United States Attorney. The Secret Service has briefed you on an investigation of David Duquesne and you must decide whether or not to prosecute him under 18 U.S.C. § 879(a)(3), which provides in relevant part: "Whoever knowingly and willfully threatens to kill, kidnap, or inflict bodily harm upon a major candidate for the office of President or Vice President, or a member of the immediate family of such candidate shall be fined under this title or imprisoned not more than 5 years, or both."

Focus on the elements of the offense set out in the statute. Here are the sequential notes you took when you reviewed the file. You culled this timeline and these facts from affidavits of agents and interview statements of witnesses. You believe that you can prove this much in court:

1. On February 10, 2007, Barack Obama was declared to be a major candidate for President under 18 U.S.C. § 3056, and was assigned Secret Service protection. He remained a major candidate for President within the meaning of 18 U.S.C. § 879 until his election as President on November 4, 2008.

2. The Defendant, David Duquesne, resides in Libertad, California.

3. On or about October 22, 2008, Defendant made the following statement on his account at the public Twitter.com website: "Re: Obama — fk the nig, he

will have a 50 cal in the head soon." He followed that tweet shortly with a tweet that said "burp, need more VINOOOO."

4. About twenty minutes later, Defendant made the following statements on his account at a public Twitter.com website: "shoot the nig" and "country fkd for 4 years+, what nig has done ANYTHING right?? long term?? never in history, except sambos." Several hours later, in response to disapproving tweets from several persons, some of which threatened to report Defendant to the authorities, he tweeted "Listen up white crybabies, I was drunk."

5. John Q. Citizen, a retired Air Force officer residing in Paradiso, California, saw the "shoot the nig" message and was concerned that the posting threatened harm to Barack Obama. On October 22, 2008, Mr. Citizen telephoned the Los Angeles Field Office of the United States Secret Service and reported the "shoot the nig" posting.

6. On October 22, 2008, a Secret Service Agent located the "shoot the nig" posting on Twitter.com. While reviewing the tweets of Duquesne, she also found the "Re: Obama" tweet.

7. When posting both statements, Defendant used the Twitter.com user name "angrywhiteguy." On October 30, 2008, Twitter.com provided the Secret Service with subscriber information for the "angrywhiteguy" account. The account was registered in the alias of "David Davis" in Libertad, California. Twitter.com also provided Internet protocol history for the account.

8. Using the Internet protocol information from Twitter.com, the Secret Service identified an IP address that it suspected may have been used to post the two messages. The Secret Service requested that Cox Cable Communications provide Internet subscriber information related to the IP address. On November 21, 2008, Cox Cable provided subscriber information revealing that the IP address was associated with an account in Libertad in the name of Sarah Duquesne, the Defendant's wife.

9. On November 21, 2008, Secret Service Agents interviewed Defendant at his residence in Libertad, California. The agents showed Defendant the "Re: Obama" message and Defendant admitted that he posted that statement from his home computer. He told them that he had been drinking that evening but he argued that even a drunken American has a right to free speech. When asked, Defendant admitted that he had weapons in the home. After the agents observed a handgun in plain sight on a shelf nearby, Defendant stated that he had additional weapons.

10. On November 25, 2008, Secret Service agents executed a federal search warrant at Defendant's residence. They found six firearms, including a Remington model 700ML .50 caliber muzzle-loading rifle. They also found a supply of .50 caliber ammunition. These items were legally seized and are admissible in evidence.

11. The Secret Service's forensic examination of the hard drive from the Defendant's home computer recovered the following messages he sent on Election Day:

> a. A November 4, 2008, email message from the Defendant to an associate with the subject header "Re: And so it begins." The email stated, "Pistol?? Dude, Josh needs to get us one of these, just shoot the nigga's car and POOF!" The email then provided an HTML link to an image of a Barrett model 82 caliber rifle referenced in the email.

> b. A November 4, 2008, email message from the Defendant to a second associate with the subject header "Re: And so it begins." The email stated: "Pistol . . . plink plink plink!! Now when you use a 50 cal on a nigga car you get this." The email provided an HTML link to a youtube.com video of a fiery exploding car.

Defendant admitted to sending those email messages to his two friends and admitted that he was sober when he did it.

C. FREE SPEECH IN PUBLIC SCHOOLS FOR TEACHERS

INTRODUCTION

It is beyond peradventure that the state may not punish a citizen for exercising the fundamental right to free speech. When the state is the employer and when the speaker is the state's employee, however, the situation is more complicated. So, it should not be surprising that the Supreme Court has developed a multi-level analysis for these public employee speech cases. Public school teachers represent one of the most numerous groups of state employees and the case reports are rife with lawsuits involving their right to free speech.

Public employees generally enjoy a more limited freedom of speech than other citizens, but they do enjoy some protection under the First and Fourteenth Amendments. In *Pickering v. Board of Education*, 391 U.S. 563 (1968), a public high school teacher was dismissed for writing a letter to the editor of a local newspaper that openly criticized the board of education for its allocation of funding between academics and athletics. The majority ruled that the teacher's criticism was protected free speech on a matter of public concern and, therefore, the teacher's dismissal violated the constitutional right to freedom of speech. The Court self-consciously balanced the interest of the government employee *qua* citizen to speak out on matters of public concern against the interest of the government *qua* employer to effectively and efficiently perform public services through its employees.

In *Connick v. Myers*, 461 U.S. 138 (1983), the Court further clarified the constitutional balance between protected speech that is a matter of public concern and unprotected speech that is related to private concerns:

> We hold only that when a public employee speaks not as a citizen upon matters of public concern, but instead as an employee upon matters only of personal interest, absent the most unusual circumstances, a federal court is not the

appropriate forum in which to review the wisdom of a personnel decision taken by a public agency allegedly in reaction to the employee's behavior. Our responsibility is to ensure that citizens are not deprived of fundamental rights by virtue of working for the government; this does not require a grant of immunity for employee grievances not afforded by the First Amendment to those who do not work for the state.

Id. at 147 (citation omitted). The Court explained that whether an employee's speech is a matter of public concern or a matter of private concern should be determined by the content, form, and context of the speech. The government employee in *Connick* was an assistant state prosecutor who was dissatisfied with the decision to transfer her to another section. She circulated a lengthy questionnaire to her colleagues asking their views of office transfer policies, morale, the need for a grievance committee, the level of confidence in supervisors, and whether they felt pressured to work in political campaigns. The official reasons given for her termination were that she had resisted the transfer and that her questionnaire was an act of insubordination. On closer analysis, the majority concluded that, except for the one question in the questionnaire regarding pressure upon employees to work in political campaigns, the rest of the questions were not matters of general public concern, constitutionally speaking. And so, the limited free speech interest attached to that one question was insufficient to immunize the assistant state prosecutor's entire questionnaire. Rather, the supervisor's decision to terminate her employment was justified by the supervisor's stated belief that the questionnaire was reasonably likely to disrupt the office by directly undermining the supervisor's authority and indirectly harming the close working relationships within the office.

The most recent Supreme Court decision in this line of public employee free speech cases, *Garcetti v. Ceballos*, 547 U.S. 410 (2006), was a game changer. Ceballos was a deputy district attorney who was asked by a defense counsel to review a case in which, the defense counsel claimed, the affidavit police used to obtain a search warrant was inaccurate. Concluding upon his review that the affidavit contained serious misrepresentations, Ceballos relayed his findings to his supervisors and followed up with a disposition memorandum recommending dismissal. His supervisors nevertheless determined that the prosecution should go forward. Later, at a hearing on a defense motion to challenge the warrant, Ceballos recounted his conclusions about the misrepresentations in the affidavit, but the trial court rejected the defense challenge and allowed the prosecution to go forward. Subsequently, Ceballos claimed that in the aftermath of these events he was subjected to a series of retaliatory employment actions, including a reassignment from his calendar deputy position to a trial deputy position, a transfer to another courthouse, and a denial of a promotion. Ceballos filed an employment grievance, but his grievance was denied. Still unsatisfied and undeterred, Ceballos did what any red-blooded American lawyer would do: he made the career decision to sue his bosses in the U.S. District Court asserting that his government employers had violated his constitutional right to free speech.

Ceballos thus went all in — and lost in the Supreme Court. The Court found that Ceballos's oral and written expressions were made pursuant to his official duties as the supervising calendar deputy and as a staff prosecutor; therefore, he was fulfilling his official responsibilities to advise his supervisors about the pending case. "We hold," the majority concluded, "that when public employees make statements pursuant to their official duties, the employees are not speaking as citizens for First Amendment purposes, and the Constitution does not insulate their communications from employer discipline." *Id.* at 421. In essence, the employee's speech is not protected by the First Amendment freedom of speech.

As summarized above, the prior cases established a two-step inquiry for a government employee who asserts a free speech claim. The constitutional question is whether the employee's speech addresses a "matter of public concern." If the answer is "no," the First Amendment provides no protection from discharge or discipline. If the answer is "yes," however, a court must proceed to balance the First Amendment interests of the public employee speaking out as a citizen on a matter of public concern against the government employer's interest in the effective and efficient fulfillment of its governmental responsibilities to the public. Significantly, *Garcetti v. Ceballos* added an antecedent inquiry preliminary to the "matter of public concern" question. If the public employee is speaking pursuant to his employment responsibilities — as part of the employee's official duties and responsibilities — the employee is speaking entirely outside the realm of the First Amendment and the government employer can have its way with him, like any private employer can have its way with any private employee. There is no *Pickering* balancing analysis because there is no constitutionally protected speech in play. Thus, this holding was a significant roll-back of the free speech rights of public employees.

EXERCISE 12.3: IS THE OUTSPOKEN TEACHER OUT OF A JOB?

SKILLS AND VALUES UTILIZED:

- Reviewing litigation documents

- Factual analysis

- Case synthesis to summarize the applicable law

- "I-R-A-C" analysis to apply the law to the facts

- Arguing the law within the summary judgment paradigm of FED. R. CIV. P. 56

ESTIMATED TIME FOR COMPLETION: Approximately 1 hour.

LEVEL OF DIFFICULTY (1 to 5):

TASK: Review the redacted versions of the Complaint and the Answer that follow these instructions. Carefully parse the factual allegations in these pleadings. Keep in mind the doctrine summarized in the Introduction. Outline your legal argument before the district court for summary judgment in favor of your client: the Milton County School District.

UNITED STATES DISTRICT COURT, S.D. AREOPAGITICA

DEBORAH A. MARTER, Plaintiff,

v.

MILTON COUNTY SCHOOL DISTRICT, et al., Defendants

No. 2012-1234

COMPLAINT AND REQUEST FOR JURY TRIAL

Plaintiff, Deborah A. Marter, by her undersigned counsel, for her claims against Defendants, states as follows:

Introduction

1. This action arises under the First and Fourteenth Amendments to the United States Constitution. In addition, this action arises under the Civil Rights Act of 1871, Title 42 U.S.C. § 1983. Defendants retaliated against Plaintiff for her exercise of her First Amendment right to free speech by subjecting her to adverse actions including, but not limited to, wrongfully discharging her from her employment with the Milton

County School District. Plaintiff's constitutional claims under the First and Fourteenth Amendments are premised upon Plaintiff's exercise of her rights of freedom of speech, expression, association, and belief, as well as her constitutionally protected right not to be retaliated against or discharged from employment on account of her exercise of her right to petition the government for the redress of grievances.

2. This action arises directly under the United States Constitution, under Title 42 U.S.C. § 1983, § 1985, and § 1988. This action also arises under the state of Areopagitica's common law and statutory law applicable to public school teachers.

Nature of this Action

3. This is an action for monetary damages, declaratory judgment, and reasonable attorney fees and costs.

Parties

4. Plaintiff, Deborah A. Marter, resides in Milton, Areopagitica.

5. Defendant, Milton County School District ("MCSD"), is a Community School Corporation organized and existing pursuant to the laws of the State of Areopagitica. Its offices are located in Milton County, Areopagitica. MCSD operates under and pursuant to the laws, policies, practices and regulations of the State of Areopagitica. MCSD acts under and pursuant to color of authority vested in it by the State of Areopagitica.

[¶¶ 6-13 are omitted.]

Factual Allegations

14. Plaintiff was hired by MCSD in September 2011 to teach in the "LAUNCHED" classroom at Clear Creek Elementary School. The LAUNCHED program was designed to provide an alternative learning experience in a multi-age setting for students of all abilities in grades 4, 5, and 6.

15. At the time she was hired, the Plaintiff was promised a position in the MCSD administration in two years provided she would accept the position in the LAUNCHED classroom, which was generally understood by all the parties to be a difficult assignment.

16. At all times relevant to this Complaint, Plaintiff performed her job duties with a level of skill and dedication consistent with Defendants' legitimate expectations.

17. On November 21, 2011, Plaintiff was observed and her performance was evaluated by the Assistant Principal at Clear Creek Elementary.

18. In the evaluation on November 21, 2011, the Assistant Principal noted the following:

> *Ms. Marter has stepped into a difficult situation, taking over a class two weeks into the school year. The previous teacher took another job and left*

abruptly. The students in the classroom are feeling abandoned as this same scenario happened to them last year. The students stay in the same class for three years with one of the intended benefits being continuity of instruction and peer group. Unfortunately, this class has had four teachers in a one year time span. They are resentful and not willing to trust. Ms. Marter is working hard to provide consistency and has high expectations for them, both academically and socially. She has remained positive and persevered with an admittedly challenging group of students as well as a group of critical parents. It is impressive to watch Ms. Marter put her vast knowledge of best practices into action. She has much to offer in methodology and life experiences.

A true, accurate, and complete copy of this evaluation is made a part hereof as *Exhibit A.*

19. On January 10, 2012, in the normal course of teaching her class, Plaintiff discussed the December 13, 2011 issue of *Time for Kids* magazine, a version of *Time* magazine geared for instructional use. It was Plaintiff's practice to read the *Time for Kids* magazine with her students in class on a weekly basis.

20. One of the articles in the December 13, 2011 issue of *Time for Kids* was a report on peace marches in Washington, D.C. protesting the wars in Iraq and Afghanistan. During the discussion, one student asked Plaintiff if she would ever march in a peace march. Although she usually did not give her opinion in class, in this case she explained that peace marches were taking place all over the country, including in Milton. She further noted that when she drove by the Milton courthouse the previous week, where the local demonstration was taking place, she honked her horn for peace, as requested by the picketers' signs. She stated to the class that she thought peace was a better option to war and that peaceful solutions should be sought before ever going to war. Plaintiff then made an analogy to the student mediators that Clear Creek Elementary School used on the playground to help children solve problems instead of fighting.

21. Shortly afterward, a female student who had recently been placed in Plaintiff's classroom for causing problems in another one told her father, in effect, that Plaintiff was against the wars in Iraq and Afghanistan.

22. The father of the female student demanded a conference with Plaintiff and the Principal of Clear Creek Elementary School both present.

23. On or about January 13, 2012, a conference was held between Plaintiff, the parents of the female student, and the Principal, at Clear Creek Elementary School.

24. Prior to the conference, Plaintiff was informed that the parents wished to discuss the LAUNCHED curriculum because they were concerned that their daughter may not be prepared for middle school. However, when Plaintiff attended the conference, it became clear that the true purpose of the conference was to discuss Plaintiff's remarks a few days earlier as described in ¶ 20 above.

25. The father of the female student accused Plaintiff of encouraging the students in her class to protest the wars in Iraq and Afghanistan. In response, Plaintiff stated that she had only discussed the *Time for Kids* article on the subject with the class, and

that the magazine was part of the approved curriculum. The father became very angry at this time, shook his finger in Plaintiff's face, and demanded that she not mention peace in her class. He stated that he supported the U.S. policy in Iraq and Afghanistan. He stated that he wanted his daughter to be a patriotic American and support the U.S. troops serving there.

26. Before Plaintiff could respond to the father, the Principal interrupted and promised him that Plaintiff would not mention peace in her class again.

27. Plaintiff complied with this directive from the Principal because she feared she would lose her job if she did not.

28. No more than one (1) day following this conference, the Principal caused to be circulated a memorandum "From the Principal" discussing "Peace at Clear Creek."

29. In the "Peace at Clear Creek" memo, the Principal noted that "We absolutely do not, as a school, promote any particular view on U.S. foreign policy related to the situation with Iraq and Afghanistan. That is not our business. Individuals in a democracy have personal beliefs, but a public school acknowledges various points of view and those might be discussed related to current events and the news."

30. A few weeks following the above-described conference and the publication of the "Peace at Clear Creek" memo, Plaintiff was given a "formal letter of concern" signed by both the Principal and the Assistant Principal, dated February 7, 2012.

31. Although no further in-class evaluations had been performed, the "formal letter of concern" advised Plaintiff to "refrain from presenting your individual personal political views."

32. From the time of the conference described in ¶¶ 23-26 above until the end of the school year, Defendants, or some of them, systematically and maliciously scrutinized and criticized Plaintiff, and undermined her efforts to perform her duties in the LAUNCHED classroom. Further, during the same time period, Defendants, or some of them, began a pattern of harassment and intimidation of Plaintiff and, in effect, attempted to set her up to fail, all in a concerted effort to retaliate against her for the statements she made in class described in ¶ 20 above.

33. On February 5, 2012, the Principal received an email from the mother of the female student described in ¶ 21 above. The email read as follows:

It seems Ms. Marter is still lecturing the class to protest the war. I have instructed my daughter that the next time this occurs I want her to report to the office immediately and ask to call home to be picked up. I have full confidence that you will support this action and comply with this request.

34. The Principal forwarded this email to Plaintiff on February 6, 2012. A true, accurate, and complete copy of this email is made a part hereof as *Exhibit B*.

35. The next day, February 7, 2012, Plaintiff was given the "formal letter of concern" described in ¶¶ 30-31 above.

36. Defendants conducted no investigation into the truth or falsity of the allegations in the email described in ¶¶ 33-34 above prior to disciplining Plaintiff based on those allegations.

37. Plaintiff prepared a formal written response to the letter of concern and circulated it to the Principal and other appropriate persons on February 9, 2012. In her response, Plaintiff pointed out that no student or parent had approached her personally with any concerns or complaints, and that neither the Principal nor the Assistant Principal had observed Plaintiff's class at any time since the formal evaluation in November 2011. Plaintiff's written response also made it clear that she had not spoken about peace in her class since teaching the *Time for Kids* article, contrary to the accusation in the email described in ¶¶ 33-34 above.

38. On February 28, 2012, Plaintiff met with the Superintendent of Defendant MCSD to ask for his help in dealing with the pattern of harassment and retaliation she was experiencing.

39. The situation worsened for Plaintiff after her meeting with the Superintendent.

40. For the remainder of the school year, Plaintiff endured numerous acts of undeserved discipline, a hostile attitude from Defendant Principal and Defendant Assistant Principal, unjustified additional scrutiny of her work, and other unwarranted and retaliatory acts by Defendants.

41. The intent, motive, purpose, and effect of Defendants' actions and inactions described herein were to punish Plaintiff for her speech on a matter of public concern.

42. The determining motive of Defendants in disciplining Plaintiff, subjecting her to the above-described retaliatory acts and hostile work environment, and in ultimately deciding not to renew her employment contract, was the exercise by Plaintiff of her constitutionally-protected political and civil rights described hereinabove.

43. Defendants have established, and in disciplining and discharging Plaintiff, have implemented employment policies and practices that are arbitrary, capricious, discriminatory, and have no rational basis in fact.

44. Defendants subjected Plaintiff to their unlawful employment policies and practices in a manner depriving her of rights and privileges secured to her by the United States Constitution, federal law, state law, and the Areopagitica State Constitution.

45. But for her discipline and discharge by Defendants, Plaintiff would have continued her employment with the MCSD. Plaintiff was otherwise happy, secure, and content with her teaching job, and but for Defendants' unlawful actions, would have completed a career educating the students enrolled in the MCSD.

46. Defendants' conduct described above was committed intentionally, willfully, maliciously, recklessly, and with gross disregard of Plaintiff's federal and state rights.

47. As a direct and proximate result of Defendants' conduct, Plaintiff has been suffering, and is presently suffering, serious mental and emotional distress, anxiety, ridicule, humiliation, indignity, loss of esteem, embarrassment, harm to reputation, loss of civil and constitutional rights, loss of wages and fringe benefits, loss of future

employment prospects, and has been forced to incur attorney's fees and other expenses to redress the wrongs perpetrated against her.

Causes of Action

First Count: First Amendment Rights Under 42 U.S.C. § 1983

48. Plaintiff incorporates by reference and realleges ¶¶ 1-47.

49. Defendants disciplined Plaintiff and retaliated against her by creating a hostile work environment, and ultimately terminated her employment by refusing to renew her contract, in violation of the First and Fourteenth Amendments to the United States Constitution and Title 42 U.S.C. § 1983.

Second Count: Conspiracy Under 42 U.S.C. § 1985

50. Plaintiff incorporates by reference and realleges ¶¶ 1-47 and ¶ 49.

51. Defendants MCSD, the Superintendent, the Principal, and the Assistant Principal all conspired together to develop and implement a plan of retaliation against Plaintiff and to stifle or chill her exercise of her First Amendment rights to free speech and to petition the government for redress of grievances.

Third Count: Breach of Contract

[¶¶ 52-56 omitted.]

Fourth Count: State Law Claims

[¶¶ 57-59 omitted.]

Relief

WHEREFORE, Plaintiff, Deborah A. Marter, prays for the following relief:

A. Grant Plaintiff a sum sufficient to compensate her as determined by the evidence as compensatory or actual damages;

B. Grant Plaintiff an appropriate sum as punitive or exemplary damages;

C. Grant Plaintiff a declaratory judgment adjudging that Defendants' conduct as described in this Complaint constitutes a violation of the First and Fourteenth Amendments to the United States Constitution;

D. Reinstate Plaintiff to her position, with an award of back pay with interest, and all other lost employment benefits. In the event that the Court finds that reinstatement is not feasible, Plaintiff prays for an award of back pay and front pay;

E. Award Plaintiff reasonable attorney's fees and costs pursuant to Title 42 U.S.C. § 1988;

F. Retain jurisdiction of this action to ensure full compliance with the law, and

G. Award Plaintiff such other and further relief as the Court deems just and proper.

Date: 5 OCT. 2012
Respectfully submitted,
Ima Barrister

Ima Barrister, Areopagitica State Bar No. 54321
Attorney for Plaintiff
100 East Market Street, Suite 100
Milton, Areopagitica 66666
(555) 867-5310
ibpa@IBPA.net
[Appendices & Exhibits omitted.]

UNITED STATES DISTRICT COURT, S.D. AREOPAGITICA

DEBORAH A. MARTER, Plaintiff,

v.

MILTON COUNTY SCHOOL DISTRICT, et al., Defendants

No. 2012-1234

ANSWER

Respectfully submitted by Thurston Howell, III, Areopagitica State Bar No. 43210, Howell & Howell, P.A., Attorneys for the Defendants.

Come now the Defendants, the Milton County School District ("MCSD"), and individually: Superintendent John Malone, Principal Cheryl Black, Assistant Principal Victoria Dodgers, and Director of Human Services Pam Skylar, by counsel, and for their answer to the Plaintiff's Complaint, would state as follows:

I. *Introduction.*

1. The Defendants admit that the Plaintiff has filed this suit. The Defendants deny the remaining allegations contained in rhetorical ¶ 1 of the Plaintiff's Complaint.

2. The Defendants admit that the Plaintiff seeks to present claims under state and federal law. The Defendants deny the remaining allegations contained in rhetorical ¶ 2 of the Plaintiff's Complaint.

II. *Nature of this Action.*

3. The Defendants admit that the Plaintiff has filed this action and the Complaint speaks for itself. The Defendants deny the remaining allegations contained in rhetorical ¶ 3 of the Plaintiff's Complaint.

III. *Parties.*

[¶¶ 4-13 omitted.]

IV. *Factual Allegations.*

14. The Defendants admit the allegations contained in rhetorical ¶ 14 of the Plaintiff's Complaint.

15. The Defendants deny the allegations contained in rhetorical ¶ 15 of the Plaintiff's Complaint.

16. The Defendants deny the allegations contained in rhetorical ¶ 16 of the Plaintiff's Complaint.

17. The Defendants admit that Assistant Principal Dodgers observed the Plaintiff in her classroom during the school day on November 21, 2011. The Defendants deny the remaining allegations contained in rhetorical ¶ 17 of the Plaintiff's Complaint.

18. The Defendants admit that after Assistant Principal Dodgers observed the Plaintiff in her classroom on November 21, 2011 and prepared a "Record of Classroom Observation" of that same date, which speaks for itself. The Defendants deny the remaining allegations contained in rhetorical ¶ 18 of the Plaintiff's Complaint.

19. The Defendants are without sufficient knowledge to either admit or deny the allegations contained in rhetorical ¶ 19 of the Plaintiff's Complaint.

20. The Defendants admit that the Plaintiff inappropriately interjected her personal political views into the classroom. The Defendants deny the remaining allegations contained in rhetorical ¶ 20 of the Plaintiff's Complaint.

21. The Defendants are without sufficient knowledge to either admit or deny the allegations contained in rhetorical ¶ 21 of the Plaintiff's Complaint.

22. The Defendants admit the allegations contained in rhetorical ¶ 22 of the Plaintiff's Complaint.

23. The Defendants admit the allegations contained in rhetorical ¶ 23 of the Plaintiff's Complaint.

24. The Defendants deny the allegations contained in rhetorical ¶ 24 of the Plaintiff's Complaint.

25. The Defendants admit that the father expressed his concern that Ms. Marter's classroom behavior was inappropriate. The Defendants deny the remaining allegations contained in rhetorical ¶ 25 of the Plaintiff's Complaint.

26. The Defendants deny the allegations contained in rhetorical ¶ 26 of the Plaintiff's Complaint.

27. The Defendants deny the allegations contained in rhetorical ¶ 27 of the Plaintiff's Complaint.

28. The Defendants admit the allegations contained in rhetorical ¶ 28 of the Plaintiff's Complaint.

29. The Defendants admit the allegations contained in rhetorical ¶ 29 of the Plaintiff's Complaint.

30. The Defendants admit the allegations contained in rhetorical ¶ 30 of the Plaintiff's Complaint.

31. The Defendants admit that the "formal letter of concern" speaks for itself. The Defendants would further note that two (2) days earlier they had received and forwarded on to the Plaintiff an email from the parent of a student in her classroom indicating that "Ms. Marter is still lecturing the class to protest the war." The Defendants deny the remaining allegations contained in rhetorical ¶ 31 of the Plaintiff's Complaint.

32. The Defendants deny the allegations contained in rhetorical ¶ 32 of the Plaintiff's Complaint.

33. The Defendants admit the allegations contained in rhetorical ¶ 33 of the Plaintiff's Complaint.

34. The Defendants admit the allegations contained in rhetorical ¶ 34 of the Plaintiff's Complaint.

35. The Defendants admit the allegations contained in rhetorical ¶ 35 of the Plaintiff's Complaint.

36. The Defendants deny the allegations contained in rhetorical ¶ 36 of the Plaintiff's Complaint.

37. The Defendants are without sufficient knowledge to either admit or deny the allegations contained in rhetorical ¶ 37 of the Plaintiff's Complaint.

38. The Defendants admit that the Plaintiff met with Superintendent Malone on February 28, 2012, and expressed concern that she felt that the parents were unfairly targeting her. The Defendants deny the remaining allegations contained in rhetorical ¶ 38 of the Plaintiff's Complaint.

39. The Defendants admit that the Plaintiff's classroom performance and the parental complaints about her continued to deteriorate after she met with Superintendent Malone on February 28, 2012, which included two parents who had filed formal grievances against her for allegedly threatening and harassing two different students. The Defendants deny the remaining allegations contained in rhetorical ¶ 39 of the Plaintiff's Complaint.

40. The Defendants admit that parental complaints about the Plaintiff became a serious problem in the latter part of the 2011-12 school year, with two parents filing

formal grievances against her for allegedly threatening and harassing two different students. The Defendants deny the remaining allegations contained in rhetorical ¶ 40 of the Plaintiff's Complaint.

41. The Defendants deny the allegations contained in rhetorical ¶ 41 of the Plaintiff's Complaint.

42. The Defendants deny the allegations contained in rhetorical ¶ 42 of the Plaintiff's Complaint.

43. The Defendants deny the allegations contained in rhetorical ¶ 43 of the Plaintiff's Complaint.

44. The Defendants deny the allegations contained in rhetorical ¶ 44 of the Plaintiff's Complaint.

45. The Defendants deny the allegations contained in rhetorical ¶ 45 of the Plaintiff's Complaint.

46. The Defendants deny the allegations contained in rhetorical ¶ 46 of the Plaintiff's Complaint.

47. The Defendants deny the allegations contained in rhetorical ¶ 47 of the Plaintiff's Complaint.

V. Causes of Action.

Count I: 42 U.S.C. § 1983: U.S. Constitutional Claim.

48. The Defendants incorporate herein by reference their responses to rhetorical ¶¶ 1 - 47 of the Plaintiff's Complaint.

49. The Defendants deny the allegations contained in rhetorical ¶ 49 of the Plaintiff's Complaint.

Count II: 42 U.S.C. § 1985: Conspiracy Claim.

50. The Defendants incorporate herein by reference their responses to rhetorical ¶¶ 1 - 47 & 49 of the Plaintiff's Complaint.

51. The Defendants deny the allegations contained in rhetorical ¶ 51 of the Plaintiff's Complaint.

Count III: State Law Breach of Contract Claim.

[¶¶ 52-56 are omitted.]

Count IV: Teacher Tenure Act Claim.

[¶¶ 57-59 are omitted.]

Affirmative Defenses

1. The Plaintiff's claims, in whole or in part, are barred by the Eleventh Amendment of the United States Constitution.

[¶ 2 is omitted.]

3. To the extent the Complaint purports to state claims based on 42 U.S.C. § 1983 against the Defendants, they have not deprived the Plaintiff of any federal constitutional or statutory rights. *Daniels v. Williams*, 474 U.S. 327, 330-31 (1986).

4. The Plaintiff's claims for punitive damages under 42 U.S.C. § 1983 against the Defendant MCSD and any individual Defendant sued in his or her official capacity are barred by federal law. *Newport v. Fact Concerts, Inc.*, 453 U.S. 247, 271 (1981).

5. The Plaintiff's First Amendment claims are barred due to the fact that her speech was not on a matter of public concern. *Garcetti v. Ceballos*, 547 U.S. 410 (2006).

6. The Plaintiff's claims are barred, in whole or in part, by the state sovereign immunities set out in Areopagitica Statutes, A.S.A. § 34-13-1.

7. The Plaintiff's claims are barred, in whole or part, by her failure to comply with the notice requirements contained in the Areopagitica Tort Claims Act, A.S.A § 34-13-3.

8. Exemplary or punitive damages are barred under Areopagitica state law. A.S.A. § 34-13-4.

9. To the extent the Complaint purports to state a claim based on 42 U.S.C. § 1983, the Defendants who have been named in their individual capacities are entitled to a qualified immunity, because their actions, at all times, were taken in good faith and did not violate any constitutional rights of which a reasonable person would have known.

10. To the extent the Complaint seeks to plead a cause of action against individuals or entities other than the School Corporation, such claims are barred by the provisions of A.S.A. § 3413-3-5(a).

11. The Plaintiff's conspiracy claims under 42 U.S.C. § 1985 are barred by the intracorporate conspiracy doctrine of federal law.

WHEREFORE, the Defendants, the Milton County School District, John Malone, Cheryl Black, Victoria Dodgers, and Pam Skylar, pray that the Court find in favor of the Defendants and that the Plaintiff take nothing by way of her Complaint and for all other just and appropriate relief in the premises.

Respectfully submitted,
Thurston Howell, III

Thurston Howell, III
Areopagitica State Bar No. 43210

Howell & Howell, P.A.
Attorneys for the Defendants

D. FREE SPEECH IN PUBLIC SCHOOLS FOR STUDENTS

INTRODUCTION

In the landmark decision condemning segregated schools that announced the beginning of the end of the American apartheid known as the Jim Crow era, Chief Justice Warren declared for a unanimous Supreme Court: "Today, education is perhaps the most important function of state and local governments. Compulsory school attendance laws and the great expenditures for public school education both demonstrate our recognition of the importance of education to our democratic society." *Brown v. Board of Education*, 347 U.S. 483, 493 (1954). The government as educator must respect the free speech rights of students and teachers. Students and teachers, in turn, must have regard for the discipline and order that are expected of them and that are so essential to learning. Every student, however, can remember incidents when this official decorum broke down and school administrators sought to discipline students. In public schools, such incidents are resolved against a background understanding of the right of free speech.

The foundational case is *Tinker v. Des Moines Independent School District*, 393 U.S. 503 (1969). The Supreme Court came to the rescue of a group of students who protested America's military involvement in Vietnam by wearing black mourning armbands to school and got suspended. The Court held that their symbolic act was protected political speech closely akin to "pure speech." The majority announced, "First Amendment rights, applied in light of the special characteristics of the school environment, are available to teachers and students. It can hardly be argued that either students or teachers shed their constitutional rights to freedom of speech or expression at the schoolhouse gate." *Id.* at 506. In ruling for the students, the majority emphasized that its own independent examination of the record demonstrated that the school officials had no reason to expect a material and substantial interference with the normal functioning of the school, and in fact there was none.

The justices have returned to the schoolhouse three times since 1969. Each time they have sided with the principal and against the student, however, qualifying the soaring endorsement of student free speech they made in *Tinker* with subsequent highly pragmatic rulings.

In *Bethel School District No. 403 v. Fraser*, 478 U.S. 675 (1986), a high school student was disciplined for delivering a speech at a school wide assembly that was full of sexual double entendres — but not any of George Carlin's "Seven Dirty Words"* — which some students reacted to with hooting and yelling and graphic sexual gestures. The majority went on to characterize the speech as so "vulgar and lewd" as to

---

* *See FCC v. Pacifica Foundation*, 438 U.S. 726, 751 (1978) (appendix transcript highlighting George Carlin's comedy monologue about the list of socially taboo words).

"undermine the school's basic educational mission." *Id.* at 685. A concurring opinion characterized the speech as sophomoric and was content to defer to the discretion of school officials to prevent disruption of school educational activities and events. *Id.* at 687.

In *Hazelwood School District v. Kuhlmeier*, 484 U.S. 260 (1988), students claimed their First Amendment rights were violated by the school principal's decision to delete two articles from the high school student newspaper they edited in their journalism class. The principal objected to the first article about pregnant students at the school because the content about sexual activity and birth control was inappropriate for the younger students and because the pregnant students, while not explicitly named in the article, might be identifiable from the content. The principal objected to the second article about the effects of divorce on students because an identified student was quoted to complain about her father's conduct and the father was not afforded the opportunity either to respond to his daughter's remarks or to consent to their publication. Because of a deadline, the principal directed that the paper be published with those pages omitted, even though those pages also contained otherwise unobjectionable articles. The majority sided with the principal:

> [W]e hold that educators do not offend the First Amendment by exercising editorial control over the style and content of student speech in school-sponsored expressive activities so long as their actions are reasonably related to legitimate pedagogical concerns . . . . It is only when the decision to censor a school-sponsored publication, theatrical production, or other vehicle of student expression has no valid educational purpose that the First Amendment is so "directly and sharply implicate[d]," as to require judicial intervention to protect students' constitutional rights.

Id. at 273 (citations omitted). Of course, there is simply no way that the government could censor a real newspaper that way. *See Miami Herald Publishing Co. v. Tornillo*, 418 U.S. 241 (1974); *New York Times Co. v. United States*, 403 U.S. 713 (1971).

There things stood for almost twenty years. Then the Court decided *Morse v. Frederick*, 551 U.S. 393 (2007), which was another win for the principal and a loss for the student. Students were released from school to line up on either side of the street to watch the Olympic Torch relay pass through town. The student got suspended for unfurling a 14-foot banner reading "BONG HiTS 4 JESUS" across the street, facing the school. The majority deemed it a school event and interpreted the banner — in agreement with the principal — to either advocate or celebrate illegal drug use in direct violation of an official school board policy. The majority reviewed the precedents. The majority affirmed the *Tinker* test that "student expression may not be suppressed unless school officials reasonably conclude that it will 'materially and substantially disrupt the work and discipline of the school.' " *Id.* at 403. However, the majority reasoned that that was not the only justification for suppressing student speech. The student was not helped by either *Fraser* or *Kuhlmeier*. The majority concluded that on the facts of the case the restriction on student speech was justified given the "special characteristics of the school environment" and the compelling government interest in preventing student drug use.

In his strident dissent in *Tinker*, Justice Black predicted: "The Court's holding in this case ushers in what I deem to be an entirely new era in which the power to control pupils by the elected 'officials of state supported public schools' in the United States is in ultimate effect transferred to the Supreme Court." 393 U.S. at 515. He worried that the majority was "subject[ing] all the public schools in the country to the whims and caprices of their loudest-mouthed, but maybe not their brightest, students." *Id*. at 525. He should not have worried. Indeed, school administrators should be pleased at how the Justices have performed as constitutional hall monitors, much to the chagrin of free speech advocates.

EXERCISE 12.4: A STUDENT SUSPENSION FOR SPEECH ON THE INTERNET

SKILLS AND VALUES UTILIZED:

- Case analysis and synthesis

- Internalizing the standard for summary judgment under the Federal Rules of Civil Procedure

- Developing a legal theory of a case for trial and appeal

- Drafting a Motion for Summary Judgment

- Assessing the strengths and weaknesses of a constitutional cause of action

ESTIMATED TIME FOR COMPLETION: Approximately 1 1/2 hours

LEVEL OF DIFFICULTY (1 to 5):

TASK: What follows next is an omnibus introduction and statement of the facts for the assigned Task of drafting one or the other Motion for Summary Judgment on behalf of either (1) the plaintiff, J.B., a minor, through her parents, Thomas Barnes and Jane Barnes — or — (2) the defendants, the Green Mountain School District, *et alia*. After reviewing the factual summary, choose the side you wish to represent and then complete the draft Motion for Summary Judgment on behalf of that client. *See* FED. R. CIV. P. 56. Fill in the third section: "III. LEGAL ANALYSIS UNDER THE FIRST AND FOURTEENTH AMENDMENTS" in the following omnibus Motion.

UNITED STATES DISTRICT COURT

SOUTHERN DISTRICT OF CYBERIA

J.B., a minor,
By and through her parents
THOMAS & JANE BARNES
Plaintiff

Civil Action No. 12-2255

v.

GREEN MOUNTAIN SCHOOL DISTRICT, et alia,
Defendants

[PLAINTIFF'S/DEFENDANT'S] MOTION FOR SUMMARY JUDGMENT AND LEGAL MEMORANDUM

There being no genuine issues of material fact in this case, the [PLAINTIFF/DEFENDANT] hereby moves for a Summary Judgment under Fed. R. Civ. P. 56.

I. FACTS

The following undisputed facts entitle the [PLAINTIFF/DEFENDANT] to Summary Judgment; this statement of facts is taken from the Plaintiff's and/or the Defendant's "Statement of Uncontested Facts" both of which have been filed with this Court and are part of the record.

On March 18, 2012, a personal profile appeared on the website MySpace.com with the picture of James Maxwell, the principal of the Blue Mountain Middle School of the Defendant Blue Mountain School District, which indicated, *inter alia*, that he was a pedophile and a sex addict. This imposter profile had been created by Plaintiff J.B., a fourteen-year-old eighth-grade student at Blue Mountain Middle School and her friend K.B., also a student. The students created the profile from the home computer owned by J.B.'s parents during non-school hours. The profile did not identify Maxwell by name, but it identified him as a principal and included his picture which had been taken from the School District's website.

The profile described its subject as a forty year old, married, bisexual man living in Florida. His interests were described as: "detention, being a tight ass, riding the Fraintrain, spending time with my child (who looks like a gorilla), baseball, my golden pen, fucking in my office, hitting on students and their parents." It also indicated that he likes television and mainly watches "the Playboy Channel on DirecTV, OH YEAH BITCH!" (emphasis in original). A statement on the profile with the heading "HELLO CHILDREN!" read as follows:

> Yes. It's your oh so wonderful, hairy, expressionless, sex addict, fat ass, put on this world with a small dick PRINCIPAL come to myspace so I can pervert the minds of other principals to be just like me. I know, I know, you're all thrilled. Another reason I came to myspace is because I am keeping an eye on you students (who I care for so much). For those who want to be my friend, and aren't in my school, I love children, sex (any kind), dogs, long walks on the beach, tv, being a dick head and last but not least my smoking wife who looks like a man (that satisfies my needs) my sexy FRAINTRAIN. So please feel free to add me, message me, and whatever.

The address or "URL" for the profile includes the phrase "kids rock my bed." Although the students created the profile at J.B.'s home, news of it soon spread to the school. The next day students were already discussing the website at school, and K.B. told five to eight students about the profile. Additionally, five or six students approached K.B. and inquired about the profile. Discussion of the website continued through the day, and there was a general "buzz" in the school with quite a few people knowing about it.

Plaintiff J.B. asserts that approximately 24 hours after the profile was created it was reset to "private." A MySpace profile set to "private" may only be viewed by those who receive permission from the profile's creator. After it was made private, J.B. and K.B. granted access to twenty-two individual fellow students to view the profile. Plaintiff asserts that the profile was set to private "approximately" one day after it was created. One day after its creation would have been Monday, March 19, 2012. Maxwell, however was evidently able to access the site on his work computer on the morning of Wednesday, March 21, 2012.

The subject of the imposter profile, Principal Maxwell, heard about it first on Monday, March 19, 2012. The next day, he was informed that the profile contained very disturbing comments about him. On that same day, at least one teacher approached Maxwell to inform him that students were discussing the profile in class.

On the following day, Wednesday, March 21, 2012, a student provided Maxwell with a complete printout of the profile. Maxwell also learned on that day that J.B. and K.B. were involved with the creation of the profile.

J.B. was absent from school on March 21, 2012. The next day, Maxwell called her to the office and met with her in the presence of the guidance counselor, Michelle Gustafson. Initially, J.B. denied any involvement with the imposter profile. Eventually, however, she admitted that she had created it with K.B. Maxwell then spoke with the parents of both J.B. and K.B. regarding the profile. He also contacted MySpace.com to have the profile removed.

Based upon the creation of the imposter profile, Maxwell determined that J.B. had violated the school discipline code, which prohibits the making of false accusations against school staff members. He found it was also a violation of the School District's computer-use policy, which informs students that they cannot use copyrighted material without permission from the agency or website from where they obtained it. This policy was violated according to the Defendant School District because the students had obtained the photo of Maxwell from the School District's website and the School District has the sole permission to use and display photographs contained on that website.

Plaintiff J.B. received a ten (10) day out-of-school suspension because she had created the website. (K.B. received the same punishment but she is not involved in this lawsuit.) During the suspension, J.B.'s school assignments were brought to her home. Prior to this incident, J.B.'s only other prior disciplinary matters had been in December 2011 and February 2012 for dress code violations. Plaintiff J.B. had the opportunity to appeal her suspension to the school superintendent and then to the school board. She did not take advantage of her opportunity to appeal her suspension.

II. PROCEDURAL HISTORY

Plaintiff instead instituted the instant lawsuit pursuant to Title 42, Section 1983 of the United States Code; subject matter jurisdiction is based on Title 28, Section 1331 of the United States Code.

Upon filing the complaint, Plaintiff also filed a motion for temporary restraining order and preliminary injunction. The District Court denied the motion for temporary restraining order and preliminary injunction on March 29, 2012, and the case proceeded through discovery. At the close of discovery, both the Plaintiff and the Defendants moved for summary judgment, bringing the case to its present posture. During the briefing of the opposing motions for summary judgment, the Plaintiff stipulated to the dismissal of the two individual Defendants, Principal Maxwell and School District Superintendent Roberta Robertson. Thus, the only Defendant remaining is the Green Mountain School District.

III. LEGAL ANALYSIS UNDER THE FIRST AND FOURTEENTH AMENDMENTS

*   *   *

[Your Task is to draft this portion of the Motion for the side you choose to represent.]

*   *   *

WHEREFORE, [PLAINTIFF/DEFENDANT] respectfully requests that this Court grant this motion for a summary judgment and enter a final judgment accordingly.

L. W. Student

L. W. Student

Attorney for [PLAINTIFF/DEFENDANT]

Chapter 13

THE ESTABLISHMENT CLAUSE

INTRODUCTION

The First Amendment provides "Congress shall make no law respecting an establishment of religion." U.S. Const., amend. I. The individual right to be free of religious establishments was incorporated and applied to the states through the Fourteenth Amendment in *Everson v. Board of Education*, 330 U.S. 1 (1947). In the opinion for the Court that established the constitutional baseline, Justice Black famously proclaimed:

> The "establishment of religion" clause of the First Amendment means at least this: Neither a state nor the Federal Government can set up a church. Neither can pass laws which aid one religion, aid all religions, or prefer one religion over another. Neither can force nor influence a person to go to or to remain away from church against his will or force him to profess a belief or disbelief in any religion. No person can be punished for entertaining or professing religious beliefs or disbeliefs, for church attendance or non-attendance. No tax in any amount, large or small, can be levied to support any religious activities or institutions, whatever they may be called, or whatever form they may adopt to teach or practice religion. Neither a state nor the Federal Government can, openly or secretly, participate in the affairs of any religious organizations or groups and vice versa. In the words of Jefferson, the clause against establishment of religion by law was intended to erect "a wall of separation between Church and State."

Id. at 15-16 (citation omitted). Ever since, separationists and accomodationists have fought over the meaning and significance of Thomas Jefferson's famous and controversial metaphor that the First Amendment erected a "wall of separation" between church and state.

The default doctrine for determining violations of the Establishment Clause is the three-pronged *Lemon* test, established in the case by the same name. "First, the statute must have a secular legislative purpose; second, its principal or primary effect must be one that neither advances nor inhibits religion; finally, the statute must not foster 'an excessive government entanglement with religion.'" *Lemon v. Kurtzman*, 403 U.S. 602, 612-13 (1971) (citations omitted). This rubric is designed to preserve the "wall of separation" against "'sponsorship, financial support, and active involvements of the sovereign in religious activity.'" *Id.* at 612. The *Lemon* test has been controversial and continues to be controversial. Various justices have called for its overruling; subsequent majorities have deployed the test in some decisions and ignored the test in other decisions. But it remains "good law."

Obviously, profound concerns for the values underlying the Establishment Clause are implicated when school officials impose a formal prayer on students attending public schools under compulsory education laws. In *Engel v. Vitale*, 370 U.S. 421 (1962), the Supreme Court struck down a board of education's policy that required students in New York to recite the following prayer at the beginning of each school day: "Almighty God, we acknowledge our dependence on Thee, and we beg Thy blessings upon us, our parents, our teachers and our Country." *Id.* at 422. The Court held that "the constitutional prohibition against laws respecting an establishment of religion must at least mean that in this country it is no part of the business of government to compose official prayers for any group of the American people to recite as a part of a religious program carried on by government." *Id.* at 425. Likewise, in *School District of Abington Township v. Schempp*, 374 U.S. 203 (1963), the Supreme Court struck down two state laws: a Pennsylvania statute that required ten verses of the Bible to be read without comment at the opening of each school day and a Maryland statute that required the reading of a chapter in the Bible without comment or the recitation of the Lord's Prayer at the beginning of the school day.

There things remained until the Supreme Court decided *Wallace v. Jaffree*, 472 U.S. 38 (1985), the point of departure for the next Exercise. The father of three public school children filed a complaint against various local school officials and Alabama state officials challenging the constitutionality of an Alabama school prayer and meditation statute. The Supreme Court held that the Alabama statute, Ala. Code § 16-1-20.1 (1981), authorizing a daily period of silence in public schools for meditation or voluntary prayer was an endorsement of religion lacking in any saving secular purpose, and thus was a law respecting an establishment of religion in violation of the First and Fourteenth Amendments. An examination of the legislative history revealed a "smoking gun" purpose and intent on the part of the sponsor and supporters of the statute to return prayer to the public school. Indeed, the sponsor tellingly eschewed any secular purpose whatsoever, testifying in the district court: "No, I did not have no [sic] other purpose in mind." 472 U.S. at 57.

A close reading of the opinions, however, may suggest how a state legislature might draft and implement a moment of silence policy that would survive constitutional scrutiny. First, Justice Stevens' majority opinion was careful to recite that the previously-enacted Alabama statute that provided for a 1-minute period of silence in all public schools "for meditation" was not before the Court for decision. 472 U.S. at 40-41. Second, Justice O'Connor wrote a separate opinion concurring in the judgment that provides some basis for believing that a properly drafted moment of silence law could pass constitutional muster. (Focus on her opinion for the next Exercise.)

EXERCISE 13.1: DRAFTING AND IMPLEMENTING A "MOMENT OF SILENCE" STATUTE

SKILLS AND VALUES UTILIZED:

- Case analysis

- Legislative drafting

- Client advising

- Litigation avoidance

ESTIMATED TIME FOR COMPLETION: Approximately 1 hour

LEVEL OF DIFFICULTY (1 to 5):

TASK 1: You are counsel to the Committee on Education of the State Senate. The Chair of the Committee has asked you to prepare a bill for committee markup that would mandate that public school students observe a 90-second period of silence for meditation or voluntary prayer at the start of each school day. Your instructions are explicit: the proposed statute must comport with Supreme Court cases so that it will survive a constitutional challenge.

TASK 2: You are the attorney for the local public school board. The board asks you to draft an explanatory statement which will be printed on little cards — like the *Miranda* warning cards police use — and distributed to homeroom teachers in the district. All teachers will be required to read the explanatory statement instructing students what to do and how to behave under the new statute you have drafted to perform Task 1 above. The members of the board want to make sure that the teachers in the school district follow the law and respect the rights of students.

Chapter 14

THE FREE EXERCISE CLAUSE

INTRODUCTION

Laws "prohibiting the free exercise [of religion]" violate the guarantees of religious liberty protected by the First and Fourteenth Amendments. The 18th century purpose was to put an end to the history of religious persecution at the hands of government, which had plagued the Old World and the colonies. The Supreme Court long has distinguished between the freedom of belief and the freedom to act: "Congress was deprived of all legislative power over mere opinion, but was left free to reach actions which were in violation of social duties or subversive of good order." *Reynolds v. United States*, 98 U.S. 145, 164 (1878). Freedom of belief is an absolute right of conscience. The freedom to act on individual beliefs cannot be absolute in a democratic and majoritarian system of self-government. Otherwise, every individual conscience would be beyond the rule of law. Thus, judicial balancing is necessary and inevitable.

Prior to 1990, the modern Supreme Court applied a version of strict scrutiny balancing in free exercise cases and the religionists more often than not were granted constitutional exemptions from general laws that burdened the practice of their religion. *See Wisconsin v. Yoder*, 406 U.S. 205 (1972) (Old Order Amish were excused from the state's compulsory school-attendance law); *Sherbert v. Verner*, 374 U.S. 398 (1963) (s Sabbatarian could not be denied unemployment compensation for refusing to work on Saturday). The free exercise of religion was deemed a fundamental right and laws that burdened that right were subjected to strict scrutiny judicial review.

In *Employment Division v. Smith*, 494 U.S. 872 (1990), the majority recalibrated the judicial balancing analysis significantly. An otherwise valid law of general applicability that is neutral will be deemed constitutional even though the law has an incidental effect of burdening a particular religious practice. In that case, for example, the majority upheld the state law denying unemployment benefits to persons who were dismissed from their jobs as drug counselors because they had ingested peyote (a hallucinogen on the list of controlled substances) during a traditional and authentic religious ceremony of the Native American Church. This 5-to-4 decision was vigorously contested by the dissenters and a consensus of commentators criticized the shift in emphasis announced by the majority, but *Smith* remains "good law," as we lawyers say. The free exercise of religion is currently understood to be a comparative right: how the government must treat religious practices now is defined by how the government treats comparable secular practices.

The corollary rule, necessary to protect religious exercise from untoward government hostility and improper political agendas, was announced in the next landmark case: *Church of the Lukumi Babalu Aye, Inc. v. City of Hialeah*, 508 U.S. 520 (1993). Laws that target religious practices are neither neutral nor generally applicable; an anti-religious motive on the part of lawmakers will render a law unconstitutional. For all intents and purposes, the city council of Hialeah, Florida, enacted ordinances with the invidious purpose to prohibit the animal sacrifice rituals of the Santeria religion. Consequently, the Supreme Court easily declared those ordinances unconstitutional without a dissenting opinion. Laws are subject to the compelling interest test if they overtly discriminate against religion, if they are enacted because of an anti-religious motive, or if their anti-religious effect is exclusive or dominant instead of merely incidental. The Hialeah ordinances had nothing going for them besides community disapproval of Santeria practices and hostility towards its practitioners.

Thus, lawmakers must carefully steer between the Scylla and Charybdis of *Smith* and *Lukumi* to avoid having their laws declared unconstitutional under the Free Exercise Clause.

EXERCISE 14.1: PROVIDING A LEGAL OPINION ABOUT A PROPOSED "DRIVEWAY FEE"

SKILLS AND VALUES UTILIZED:

- Case analysis and synthesis
- Client advising
- Plain language communication
- Litigation avoidance

ESTIMATED TIME FOR COMPLETION: Approximately 1 1/2 hours

LEVEL OF DIFFICULTY (1 to 5):

TASK: You are the City Attorney for the City of Eden. Draft your presentation for the next meeting of the City Council that explains the law of the Free Exercise Clause as it would apply to the proposed driveway fee, which is described in detail in the email reproduced below. The members are not lawyers, so you cannot rely on legal jargon such as "strict scrutiny" that you might use in court before a judge. You must speak in plain language, but you must convey the substance of the doctrine that the Supreme Court has developed and a trial court would apply. Anticipate their questions. You can expect the Mayor to stubbornly insist that her idea is a good idea and you will have to overcome her stubbornness. She will not accept the lazy lawyer's answer "because we will get sued and we will lose" because she is feeling political pressure to increase revenues in order to provide basic public services to residents. And she believes that the driveway fee would be comparably more fair than the present property tax system. You must persuade her and her colleagues to do the right thing — the constitutional thing.

ROLE PLAYING: You hit on the idea of preparing your presentation and practicing it on someone who is not a lawyer, e.g., a relative or a friend, to see how it goes. Find someone who is not a lawyer or a law student and rehearse it live and in person. Allow him or her to ask questions and respond in character. Yes. Really do this. Then de-brief the person to evaluate how successful you were in explaining the law in terms understandable to a layperson.

BACKGROUND INFORMATION: The mayor sends you the following email which contains the details of her idea to raise needed revenues for the City:

Email to City Attorney L.W. Student

From: Mayor Eve Adams

Re: driveway fee

As you know, Eden depends on property taxes for budget revenues and we currently are struggling to balance our budget to be able to afford basic municipal services. Ninety percent of all parcels in the city pay less than $100 a year in property taxes. Sixty percent of all commercial properties pay less than $1,000 a year in property taxes. But all the church properties — including places of worship, schools, and community centers — are exempt from local property taxes under the controlling state law. We have so many churches in Eden, however, that a significant percentage of the real property in the city is not taxed at all. This is a revenue problem. It is a cost problem, as well. We have to deploy police to direct traffic outside several of the larger churches before, during, and after their regularly scheduled services on Wednesdays and Sundays and that runs up costly overtime wages for the officers. We have to find a way to make churches pay their fair share.

I found an idea on the Internet that will help solve this problem: a driveway fee. Here is how it would work:

- The "driveway fee" is not a tax. It is a user fee, assessed through property tax bills.

- The concept is simple: the more traffic a property generates, the more that property contributes towards general city revenues that go towards maintaining roads and sidewalks and providing traffic police, etc. This is similar to other public utility fees, such as storm sewers and water service. The fee is not tied to fluctuations in property tax valuations or sales tax collections.

- All developed properties would pay the fee, which would include otherwise tax-exempt religiously-owned properties such as schools and churches and temples. The fee would be collected via property tax assessments; consequently, they would be sent to property owners, not tenants. However, a property owner could elect to pass the fee on to tenants.

- The fee would be calculated by estimating the average number of vehicle trips each property within the City generates and assessing a fee based on the intensity (type/size) of the use. The more trips generated by a particular property, the higher the driveway fee assessment. The City would rely on studies compiled by an independent association called the Institute of Transportation Engineers contained in a publication titled *The Trip Generation Manual*. Developers frequently utilize this *Manual* to compute appropriate parking lot sizes for new developments based on trip generation rates. No actual traffic counts would be taken on any parcel in our City. We would use the neutral national statistics to calculate the driveway fee for each parcel.

- Property owners would be permitted to appeal the land use classification of their property and request a change in its classification, but the owner must demonstrate that their property should be classified according to a different use category. For example, an owner of an industrial site classified as a "General Office Building," might appeal to be classified as a "General Light Industrial" site.

- Single family homes would pay a flat fee of $72 per year. For commercial properties, the fee would depend on the land use type (e.g., retail, office, etc.), the building size, and the number of parking spaces. The fee would be calculated based on tables estimating the frequency of visits. A convenience store might have only a few parking spaces but frequent customers per space per day while a big box store like Wal-Mart might have many parking spaces but fewer customers per space per day. The *Manual* has tables for all these different factors.

- The *Manual* estimates 5.8 weekly vehicle trips for every worship seat in the religious facility. For the largest Protestant churches in the city, therefore, the annual fee would be between $1,000 and $1,500. Smaller congregations would pay less.

- Of course, the driveway fee would not be limited only to church-owned property. In this way it is fair and equal. I go to church every Sunday and I would not object as a church goer to my congregation having to pay our fair share for the municipal services we utilize.

Of course, the devil is always in the details. I request that you brief the City Council at our next meeting on how we can legally implement a driveway fee in the City of Eden. Give this your highest priority. Don't bore us or confuse us with legalese and don't go on and on. Be brief and entertain questions.